THE HISTORY OF
WORLD
EVENTS

For Max Longley

First published in 2003 by Armadillo Books
An imprint of Bookmart Limited
Blaby Road, Wigston
Leicestershire, LE18 4SE, England

ISBN 1-84322-070-9

Production by Omnipress, Eastbourne

Printed in Singapore

THE HISTORY OF
WORLD
EVENTS

RODNEY CASTLEDEN

CONTENTS

INTRODUCTION

The Great Sphinx and the Pyramids of Giza.

THE STORY OF the human race may be compared to a river, or the voyage of a ship across an ocean, an endless flow of events, each one leading continuously into the next. It is a long chain of actions and results, causes and effects, but it is also clear that the human story sometimes moves forward in quite sudden surges or spasms. Every so often there is a major event, such as the outbreak of war, that throws whole communities, sometimes whole continents, into turmoil. These events, which are the focus of this book, produce step-changes in everyone's lives.

Napoleon Bonaparte 1769–1821.

Some step-changes may happen as a result of a chance discovery, some as a result of human ingenuity or invention, some as a result of the will to power of a particular individual or group of people. When we look closely, we find that the changes sometimes come about in unexpected ways. There has been debate recently, for instance, about whether Christopher Columbus really 'discovered' America. It has been suggested that the Atlantic had already been crossed and the New World was already known and Columbus's 1492 voyage was stage managed, rather in the style of an official opening ceremony.

Some changes have resulted from the actions of individual people. The great nineteenth century historian Thomas Carlyle believed that 'the History of the world is but the biography of great men', and many subsequent history books have been written from that standpoint, with a focus on the life stories of explorers like Columbus, inventors like Watt, or military leaders like Napoleon. Yet there are often background processes that move things forward and prepare the way for great events.

James Watt's steam engine, circa 1775.

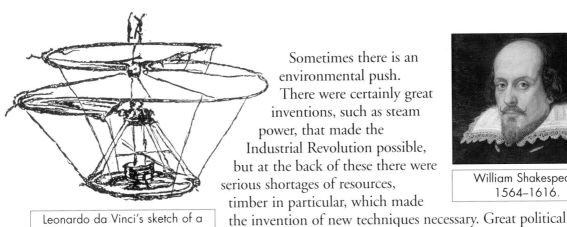

Leonardo da Vinci's sketch of a flying machine, circa 1500.

Sometimes there is an environmental push. There were certainly great inventions, such as steam power, that made the Industrial Revolution possible, but at the back of these there were serious shortages of resources, timber in particular, which made

William Shakespeare 1564–1616.

the invention of new techniques necessary. Great political changes like the French Revolution were certainly moved forward by the writings of Rousseau and the actions of charismatic leaders like Danton and Robespierre, but behind them were serious economic crises and glaring inequalities between the life styles of the rich and the poor.

Erupting into the human story from time to time like volcanic islands are the great civilizations, each one representing a new and original way for people to live their lives. It seems useful for the purposes of this book to treat the eruption of these cultural volcanoes as world events too.

War is an obvious agent of change in people's lives and in the lives of entire nations, and it always involves huge costs, unbearable losses and terrible suffering. To understand the past - and to prepare ourselves for the future - we need to understand the causes as well as the effects of wars. History has important things to tell us about ourselves and what may happen to us. We need to learn from the mistakes of the past. The 'lesson of history' has been referred to repeatedly since the poet Coleridge first put it into words in 1831:

'If men could learn from history, what lessons it might teach us! But passion and party blind our eyes, and the light which experience gives is a lantern on the stern, which shines only on the waves behind us!'

Execution of Louis XVI during the French Revolution, January 21, 1793.

7

THE
ANCIENT WORLD

The First 'Modern' People

40,000 BC

OVERVIEW ❖ OVERVIEW ❖ OVERVIEW ❖ OVERVIEW ❖ OVERVIEW

There have been man-like creatures for 3 million years, but it was only in 38,000 BC that people like us emerged, with brains that functioned like ours, and the ability to create art – and probably language too.

The Emergence of Man

The earliest man-like creatures, or hominids, are known as Australopithecines. Advanced types known as *Homo erectus* (upright man) could make tools out of stone, walk upright and make fire, but their brains were very small. The earliest true humans, known as *Homo habilis* (handy man), appeared in Africa around two million years ago. The Neanderthals, a species much closer to modern people and known as *Homo sapiens*, appeared 200,000 years ago; they were well adapted to living in a cold climate and were able to colonize a northern Europe that was

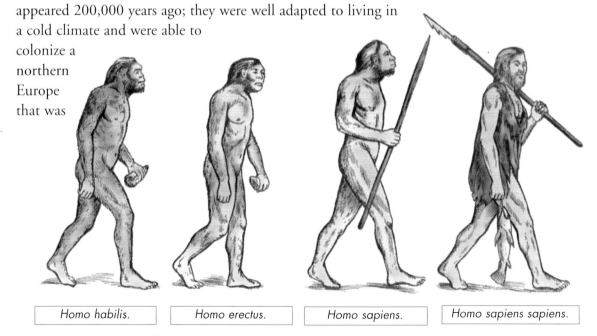

| Homo habilis. | Homo erectus. | Homo sapiens. | Homo sapiens sapiens. |

| **TIME LINE** | 40,000 BC | 10,000 | 5000 | 4000 | 500 | AD1 | 200 | 400 |

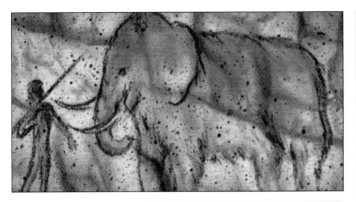

Cave paintings have proved to be a valuable source of information about prehistoric life.

subject to ice cover in repeated glaciations. The first 'modern' people, *Homo sapiens sapiens*, appeared about 38,000 years ago.

35,000 years ago, when the sea level was low, people crossed from Asia to North America by way of the Bering Straits land bridge. Shortly afterwards the first people arrived in Australia, also from Asia, also via a land bridge, but they must have travelled part of the way by boat.

Homo sapiens sapiens: 'Wise, wise man'

These new people had the ability not only to make shelter and clothing, but to make artefacts, some of them quite elaborate. They made art too. Painted images, such as those in the caves at Lascaux in France, show the animals they liked to hunt. These pictures may have been to do with hunting magic. People hunted in groups, chasing large animals such as bison and mammoths, and driving them into ravines or off cliffs to kill them for their meat and skins.

Some of the bone, tusk and antler was used to make carvings, including engravings and figurines of reindeer, bison and horses. The ivory head of a woman carved in France 25,000 years ago may be the world's first portrait.

CHRONOLOGY OF EVENTS
130,000 – 8000 BC

130,000 BC
Neanderthals in Asia.

60,000 BC
Probable arrival of modern people (*Homo sapiens*) in Australia.

38,000 BC
Modern people (*Homo sapiens sapicus*) in Africa, Europe and Asia.

30,000 BC
Stone tools in use in Japan.

26,000 BC
Ritual cremation in Australia.

15,000 BC
Cave wall paintings made at Lascaux, Chauvet and Cosquer in France.

12,000 – 8000 BC
Ice Age land bridge between Asia and Alaska allowed at least three waves of migration from Siberia to America (Palaeo-Indian, Na-Dene, then Aleut-Eskimo migrations).

A selection of stone points and bone tools, which would have been used for carvings and engravings.

The First Farmers

8000 BC

OVERVIEW ❖ OVERVIEW ❖ OVERVIEW ❖ OVERVIEW ❖ OVERVIEW

Farming began in the Middle East shortly after 10,000 years ago. People began to domesticate the plants and animals they found useful. Permanent settlements were founded for the first time – the first villages, often consisting of solid, well-built houses.

Taming nature

Major climate warming as the last cold stage of the Ice Age ended in 10,000 BC changed every environment in middle latitudes. People became far more aware of their

Sennedjem and his wife in the fields sowing and tilling, from the Tomb of Sennedjem wall painting.

environment as it changed around them, and chose to surround themselves with the plants and animals they needed. Certain plants were chosen for domestication, such as wheat and barley. Ploughing was done with simple ploughs, called ards, tipped with antler, bone or stone; they didn't turn the soil, they merely broke it. Sickles made of flint were used for reaping.

With animals it was different. Dogs adopted people, scavenging their food scraps, in return allowing themselves to be used in hunting – and to round up other animals.

| TIME LINE | 40,000BC | 8000 BC | 5000 | 4000 | 500 | AD1 | 200 | 400 |

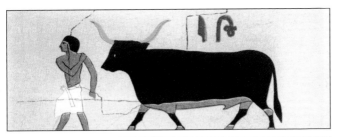

Cattle belonging to Prince Mourhet.
From drawings at Prince Mourhet's tomb at Giza.

The Fertile Crescent

The earliest farmers lived in the Fertile Crescent, which stretched from the Nile valley through Israel and Lebanon to Mesopotamia, the valleys of the Euphrates and Tigris (modern Iraq).

Farming led on to other very significant developments. People stayed in one place to be near their crops and livestock, and permanent villages were built for the first time. Permanent settlements meant that it was worth investing time in building substantial houses. In Europe in 5000 BC, there were many solidly built aisled log cabins with high thatched roofs. They had indoor hearths for heating and cooking and interior walls partitioning the houses into several rooms.

Another major invention was irrigation to ensure a water supply for the new crops in the hot dry lands of the Near East. In Egypt, this consisted of networks of channels leading out from the river bank and shadufs to raise the river water over the bank.

CHRONOLOGY OF EVENTS
10,000 – 2500 BC

10,000 BC

Major climate warming as the last cold stage of the Ice Age ends.
Farming begins in the Middle East.
People begin to domesticate the plants and animals they find useful.

6000 BC

Catal Huyuk, a farming village in Anatolia, is founded.
Farming communities appear in Greece.

5000 BC

Farming begins in central Europe; farming communities live in solidly built log cabins with high thatched roofs.
Farming with irrigation systems begins in the Middle East.
Maize is cultivated in Mexico.

4800 BC

The first small-scale attempts at farming in Britain.

2300 BC

Rice is introduced into northern China from the Indus valley civilization.

2205 BC

The Chinese domesticate sheep, goats, pigs, oxen and dogs and mill grain for the first time.

The Megalith Builders of the North

5000 BC

OVERVIEW ❖ OVERVIEW ❖ OVERVIEW ❖ OVERVIEW ❖ OVERVIEW

From 5000 until 2000 BC, people living on the coasts of Western Europe built monuments out of big stones. The purpose of these standing stones, circles and tombs is hard to understand, but they were important foci for the first agricultural communities, and had religious associations with death, the sun and a goddess.

Standing stones

All along the Atlantic and Mediterranean coastline of Europe are the remains of ancient monuments made of huge stones, or 'megaliths'. Single standing stones may have been idols or territorial markers; the stone circles were temples; the chamber tombs were graves for whole communities. Often they contain deliberate alignments to sunrises or sunsets on the shortest or longest days of the year. They were important foci for their communities, who spent a lot of time building them.

They are usually associated with the first farmers. But the earliest truly megalithic monuments were built in north-western France, where the Dissignac passage graves and the

TIME LINE 40,000BC 10,000 **5000 BC** 4000 500 **AD1** 200 400

Megalithic temple site, c.30,000–c.25,000 BC, Hagar Qim, Malta.

Kercado chamber tomb were raised in about 5000 BC, just before farming began.

The biggest megalith ever raised was the gigantic standing stone in Brittany known as Le Grand Menhir Brisé. It weighed 348 tonnes and stood 20 metres high. It now lies broken in several pieces, like several other standing stones, and it seems to have been deliberately toppled in prehistoric times. The megalith builders often changed their minds about their monuments.

Malta, Stonehenge and hidden meanings

Malta has a magnificent series of megalithic temples made of dressed limestone blocks. The Tarxien temple has elaborate carved designs and a statue of a goddess.

The most famous megalithic monument is Stonehenge, made of sarsen stones dragged from 30km away and arranged in a circle surrounding five trilithons in 2400 BC. Each trilithon may have represented the doorway into a tomb chamber. The West Kennet long barrow near Avebury has five chambers arranged in this way. The overall design of the stone monument, which included bluestones from Wales, symbolizes a ruined roundhouse, a communal dwelling. Probably all megalithic architecture contains hidden symbolism of this sort.

Stonehenge, on Salisbury Plain.

Ancient Egypt
3500 BC

OVERVIEW ❖ OVERVIEW ❖ OVERVIEW ❖ OVERVIEW ❖ OVERVIEW

The rich, irrigation-based civilization of ancient Egypt lasted from 3500 BC until 30 BC (the death of Cleopatra) and beyond. Its complex, layered society was ruled by kings (pharaohs) who lived lives of great luxury. They were buried in expensive tombs with many grave-goods that tell us much about life in ancient Egypt.

Irrigation and society

The ancient Egyptian civilization developing in the Nile valley depended on an irrigation system that needed a complex political and administrative system to run it effectively. From 3100 BC Egypt was united under a single ruler, or pharaoh, who was treated as a god. There were many officials, including administrators and priests. At the bottom of this 'pyramid' society were the workers. The tombs of the rulers contain many carvings and paintings showing scenes of everyday life, including fields being ploughed with pairs of oxen.

The Great Sphinx and the Pyramids of Giza.

Pyramids

The Egyptians believed in life after death, embalmed their dead and built elaborate tombs for their rulers. Sometimes these were in artificial caves

TIME LINE	40,000BC	10,000	5000	3500 BC	500	AD1	200	400

Amenhotep IV, later known as Akhenaten, who began a new religion of Aten, the sun disc.

cut into the side of a valley, sometimes in pits covered by square single-storey buildings called mastabas. Later, to make the monument more imposing, a step pyramid was built, which was in effect a multi-storey mastaba. The final development was the true pyramid, with smoothly sloping sides.

Pharaohs

The ruler best known to us is Tutankhamun, because his tomb survived unrobbed until it was discovered in 1920, complete with his magnificent gold mask. But Tutankhamun was a minor pharaoh, murdered when he was only 18. The oddest pharaoh was Amenhotep IV, who worshipped the sun-god Ra and the Sun in the sky, Aten, changing his name to Akhenaten. He tried to convert Egypt, a culture of many gods, to the worship of a single god, but when he died Egypt turned back to its old gods.

The most famous female ruler of Egypt was Cleopatra (69–30 BC). Her reign came when the civilization was in decline, its power taken by Rome. She committed suicide in Alexandria rather than be taken to Rome as part of Augustus's triumph.

CHRONOLOGY OF EVENTS
3500 – 30 BC

3500 BC

Irrigation-based civilization of ancient Egypt began.

3100 BC

Egypt is united under a single ruler, Menes.

1801 BC

Amenhotep IV accedes to the throne.

1792 BC

Amenhotep IV, who changed his name to Akhenaten, dies.

1540 BC

Ahmose invades Nubia, fighting the Libyans and Syrians to secure Egypt's borders.

1483–1450 BC

Egypt reaches its zenith under Thutmose III.

1358 BC

Tutankhamun becomes king, aged 9.

1350 BC

Harmhab seizes the throne; Tutankhamun is killed and buried at Thebes with a vast treasure.

1237 BC

Ramesses II dies after ruling for 67 years.

30 BC

Cleopatra commits suicide.

The Ancient Religions of Egypt & Sumer

3000 BC

The deities of Egypt and Sumer are among the eldest ever recorded and therefore of an extreme archaeological as well as religious importance. Religion guided every aspect of ancient Egyptian and Sumerian life, and was based on polytheism – the worship of many deities

Ancient Egyptian religion

All civilizations have their own creation stories or myths, often involving more than one generation of gods. The Egyptians believed the world began as a watery chaos. The Sun god Atum came out of the chaos and created the gods of air and water, Shu and Tefnut, who had a daughter, the sky goddess Nut, and a son, the earth god Geb. Nut and Geb became man and wife.

There were many gods. One of the oldest was Osiris, mythical first king of the Two Lands (Upper and Lower Egypt) and king of the dead. The jackal-headed Anubis was the protector of cemeteries and weigher of the human heart at the Last Judgement. Horus was the falcon-headed sky-god and personification

Above: The process of mummification was practised throughout most of early Egyptian history. The Egyptians believed that the body contained the soul and that it must therefore be preserved to prevent the spirit being destroyed. *Left:* Anubis, god of the dead, portrayed with the head of a jackal.

TIME LINE	40,000BC	10,000	5000	3000 BC	500	AD1	200	400

CHRONOLOGY OF EVENTS
3000 – 2100 BC

3000 BC
The Epic of Gilgamesh originates at about this time.

2900 BC
The Step Pyramid is built by Imhotep at Saqqara in Egypt: the first large stone building in the world.

2675 BC
The Great Pyramid of Khufu is built at Giza.

2610 BC
The third and smallest pyramid is built at Giza.

2500 BC
The ziggurat of Ur-Nammu is built at Ur.

2100 BC
The Temple of Enlil is built at Nippur, Iraq.

of earthly kingship; the pharaohs were said to sit on the throne of Horus. Ptah

Enkidu, the rival and friend of Gilgamesh, sent by the Gods, arrives on Earth in the form of a comet.

was the patron of architects and sculptors; his wife Sekhmet was the lion-headed goddess of war and plague. The goddess Ma'at personified truth and divine order.

The Egyptians believed in life after death, mummifying their kings and princes and often providing them with funeral boats so that they could travel to the next world.

Ancient Sumerian religion

The Sumerians worshipped a host of gods and goddesses. The chief deities were Anu, god of the sky, Enlil, god of air who made all things possible, Enki, god of wisdom, and Inanna, goddess of love and war.

The Epic of Gilgamesh, dating to 3000 BC, describes a mythic flood sent by the gods to punish people. The gods warned one good man, Ut-napishtim, to build a boat and when the great flood came it destroyed everything except the boat. Ut-napishtim sent out birds to find land. Finally one of them did not return, showing that land was near; Ut-napishtim and his family were saved.

Gilgamesh and his friend Enkidu killed Huwawa, guardian of the cedar forest. The goddess Inanna sent the Bull of Heaven against them, but they killed that too. Enkidu died and Gilgamesh sought out Ut-napishtim, who gave him a magic plant guaranteeing eternal youth, but a serpent stole it. Eventually Gilgamesh was reconciled to his own mortality. 'Eternal life was not your destiny.'

Ancient Mesopotamia
5000 BC

OVERVIEW ❖ OVERVIEW ❖ OVERVIEW ❖ OVERVIEW ❖ OVERVIEW

The Tigris and Euphrates valleys (Mesopotamia = the land between the rivers) were a cradle of early civilization. Agriculture based on extensive fertile floodplains, highly organized irrigation systems and permanent settlement led on to the development of city-states ruled by powerful and war-like priest-kings.

The Sumerians

The Sumerian civilization, beginning in 5000 BC, evolved round the cultivation of the Euphrates and Tigris floodplains and the development of villages into city-states. Each city-state had its own water supply, drainage system, public buildings, royal palace and ziggurat.

The ziggurat was a step pyramid of mud brick, rising at least two stages, with staircases up and a temple on top. Here the king, who was also high priest, officiated at religious ceremonies that included sacrifices. Round the public buildings were the dwellings of ordinary people. Beyond the walls of the city were the farmers' fields. Beyond those were the marshlands. Present-day Marsh Arabs in southern Iraq still live in reed houses just as they did 5000 years ago. In 3200 BC the Sumerians devised the first writing system in the world. Thousands of clay

Excavated residential housewalls and part of the reconstructed Ziggurat at Ur.

TIME LINE	40,000BC	10,000	5000 BC	4000	500	AD1	200	400

The Hanging Gardens of Babylon were allegedly built by Nebuchadnezzar II for his wife Amyitis, who missed her homeland, Media, north-west Iran. They were grown on terraces and used water from the Euphrates River.

tablets were used to carry accounts, histories and textbooks. The Sumerians were also the first to invent the wheel, which they used to make pottery and simple wagons. Sumer reached its peak in 2800-2400 BC.

The Babylonians

In 1800 BC the Babylonians, living a little to the north of Sumer, shook off the rule of the Sumerians. The Babylonians devised a counting system based on the number 60, still used for measuring both time and angles. Nebuchadnezzar II came to power in 605 BC and reigned for 43 years, rebuilding the magnificent city of Babylon, adding the Hanging Gardens and the Ishtar Gate, which was covered with blue glazed tiles.

The Assyrians

While the Babylonians dominated southern Mesopotamia, the Assyrians dominated the north, developing a huge empire. Between 950 and 625 BC Babylon and Assyria were constantly at war. Assurbanipal, one of the great rulers of Assyria (668–627 BC), was a ruthless warrior and a great patron of the arts, with a magnificent palace at Nineveh.

CHRONOLOGY OF EVENTS
5000 – 550 BC

5000 BC

The Sumerian civilization begins.

3200 BC

Sumerians devise the first writing system in the world (pictograms).

2800 BC

Ancient Sumer reaches its peak.

2500 BC

The Sumerians develop a cuneiform script alphabet of 600 signs from the thousands of pictograms in use.

2000 BC

Decimal counting begins in Babylonia, which replaces Sumer as the dominant power in the Middle East.

1800 BC

Babylonians shake off the Sumerian rule.

605 BC

Nebuchadnezzar II king of Babylon comes to power.

588–586 BC

Nebuchadnezzar's army besieges Jerusalem and destroys the Great Temple of Jerusalem.

560 BC

Evil-Merodach, king of Babylon, is killed by dissidents after he releases Jehoiakim, the king of Judah who was imprisoned in Babylon for 36 years.

Ancient Crete

2500 BC

The Minoan civilization was the very first European civilization, beginning in 2500 BC. Drawing its wealth from trading by sea, this civilization produced cities with great temple-complexes and high-status priestesses. One of the religious rituals was the bull dance, which may have culminated in sacrifice.

Cities and temples

The bronze age civilization on Crete, based on farming (olive and wine production) and trading by sea, reached its peak between 2000 BC and 1400 BC. Village life based on farming evolved into city life based on food surpluses, craft industries and trading. Cities like the capital, Knossos, were laid out with stone-paved streets, drains and great buildings that were dominated by religious ceremonies, the temples (or 'palaces' as some call them). The maze-like temples were richly decorated with murals depicting the bull dance, evidently a religious ritual that took place in the central court of the temple, and processions of worshippers bringing offerings to a high priestess in the role of a goddess. The offerings were probably a compulsory tribute – taxation in all but name. The maze-like layout of Knossos gave rise to the legend of Theseus and the Minotaur.

Linear A and Linear B scripts

The Minoans, as the excavator of Knossos Sir Arthur Evans named them, had their own language and their own script, Linear A, which has yet to be deciphered. Each symbol represents a syllable rather than a letter. The later clay tablets, dating from the final stage of the civilization, are written in Linear B,

TIME LINE　40,000BC　10,000　5000　2500 BC　500　AD1　200　400

The remains of the palace at Knossos in Crete.

which is an early form of Greek. These temple archives contain lists of offerings to gods and goddesses, of which there were many. Some tablets refer to 'da-pu-ri-to-jo po-ti-ni-ja', 'The Lady of the Labyrinth' the goddess of the place.

A trading empire

The wealth of the Minoans, who called themselves Kefti, came from the sea. They were shipbuilders and navigators, travelling to other islands round the Aegean Sea with cargoes of pottery and metal work This advanced civilization, in which some women, the priestesses, held very high status, went into decline after the eruption of Santorini in about 1520 BC. Knossos fell in 1380 BC.

Polychrome Pottery, from the Palace of Minos at Knossos.

| 600 | 800 | 1000 | 1200 | 1400 | 1600 | 1800 | 1900 | 2000 |

Mycenae & the Trojan War
1600 BC

OVERVIEW ❖ OVERVIEW ❖ OVERVIEW ❖ OVERVIEW ❖ OVERVIEW

Homer, writing in 800 BC, had access to a long oral tradition reaching back to an earlier civilization. His story of a Mycenaean attack on Troy is probably loosely based on historical events. This war-like Mycenaean civilization was centred on trade and rivalry between neighbouring city-states, each with its own fortress. When the Minoan civilization collapsed, the Mycenaeans took over its trading operation.

Warrior kings

Mycenae was the citadel of a bronze age city-state in southern Greece, not on the coast but set back among hills for safety, like Knossos. The civilization grew steadily from 1600 BC onwards, often borrowing ideas for art and architecture from the contemporary Minoan civilization on Crete. Villages feeding on fertile plains expanded into cities, which then fed on each other. Initially the warrior-kings were buried in rich graves called Shaft Graves. Later on they were buried in even more opulent style in stone-built chambers with impressive beehive vaults, entrance passages and big covering mounds (tholos tombs). One tomb at Mycenae, known as the Treasury of Atreus, has a doorway 6m high and a cavernous chamber 13 metres high.

This powerful warrior culture produced heavily fortified citadels, such as Gla, Tiryns and Mycenae.

The Siege of Troy.
According to legend, the Greeks built a giant wooden horse with a hollow belly in which a number of Greek soldiers hid. The horse was left outside the gates of Troy as a supposed gift of peace. The Trojans pulled the horse within their walls, and began to celebrate the end of the war and their victory over the Greeks. At nightfall, when the whole city was in drunken uproar, the Greeks jumped from the horse, opened the gates to their own army and ransacked the city of Troy, killing all men and boys and enslaving the women and girls.

The Mycenaean empire

After the decline of the Minoan civilization from 1500 onwards, the mainland Greeks reached out and took over the Aegean trading operation. The legendary Trojan War may contain memories of a real military expedition by the Mycenaeans led by King Agamemnon against Troy, which was in a strategic position controlling access to the Black Sea. The Trojan War was fought in 1193 BC. On his return home to Mycenae, Agamemnon was murdered by his wife's lover, Aegisthos (according to Homer), and the east wing of the royal palace was set on fire (according to archaeologists).

The Mycenaean civilization itself collapsed shortly afterwards, in around 1100 BC. It is not known why, but internal political and economic problems seem likely causes.

2600 BC

An early bronze age settlement is founded at Mycenae.

1600 BC

The beginning of the Mycenaean (Late Helladic) civilization.
Invention of new burial practices: shaft graves, tholos tombs, chamber tombs.

1400 BC

The Mycenaean civilization becomes the dominant civilization in the Aegean, displacing the Minoan civilization.

1380 BC

Fall of Cretan capital Knossos, some believe as a result of Mycenaean conquest.

1350 BC

Perseus, legendary founder of Mycenae, may have lived. Perseus is the founder of the first royal dynasty at Mycenae.
The first fortress walls are built at Mycenae.

1240 BC

Mycenaeans are trying to destabilize western Anatolia. The Athenian acropolis is strongly fortified. The fortress at Mycenae is enlarged and the Lion Gate is built.

1193 BC

The Trojan War. The Mycenaeans, led by King Agamemnon, defeat the Trojans.

1190 BC

Civil war or revolution in the fortress centres. According to legend, Agamemnon is murdered on his return from Troy. The civilization declines and eventually collapses in 1100 BC.

600	800	1000	1200	1400	1600	1800	1900	2000

Early China: the Shang & Qin Dynasties

1500 BC

The great river floodplains of Eastern China were a cradle of several early civilizations. The Shang dynasty created an early empire in the valleys of the Yellow and Yangtze Rivers. In 221 BC, the famous Qin emperor, later buried with his terracotta army, created an even larger empire protected by the Great Wall of China.

The Shang dynasty

The earliest civilizations in China grew up, like the Egyptian and Sumerian civilizations, on the fertile floodplains of great rivers: the Huang He (Yellow River), the Chang Jiang (Yangtze River) and the Xi Jiang (West River). Farmers relied on the rivers to water their crops and for navigation.

The first dynasty we know about with any certainty is the Shang, which ruled in China in 1500 BC. The first Shang emperor was called T'ang. The people

At 6,000 km long, the Great Wall of China is the longest structure ever built. It was built entirely by hand, by a workforce of almost 1,000,000 people.

TIME LINE	40,000BC	10,000	5000	4000	1600 BC	AD1	200	400

cultivated millet, wheat and rice, kept sheep, dogs, chicken and cattle, and hunted wild boar and deer. They also used horses to draw ploughs and chariots. They were expert metal workers, casting elaborately decorated bronze vessels for religious ceremonies.

The Qin dynasty

A powerful warrior dynasty, the Qin (or Ch'in) emerged in north-western China. By 221 BC it had established the empire from which China takes its name. Shu Huangdi, the first emperor, organized the government so that everything was under his control. Weights were standardized; a single currency was introduced. He also tried to destroy the writings of Confucius and all other writings that were not about the Qin; this is called the 'Burning of the Books'.

Shu Huangdi ordered the building of the Great Wall (214–204 BC), to protect his empire. When the Great Wall was finished it would stretch almost 6,000 km along the northern frontier. When Shu Huangdi died aged 49 in 210 BC, a huge tomb complex was built at Xianyang to house his body and possessions; it was guarded by a life-size army of terracotta soldiers and horses. Shortly after his death the Qin dynasty was overthrown and China broke up into several small states, but the idea of a united China had been born.

The amazing army of thousands of Terracotta Warriors has been standing guard over Emperor Qin Shu Huangdi's tomb for more than 2000 years.

1500 BC
The Shang dynasty begins, and with it the first historical period in China.

1122 BC
The armies of Wu Wang defeat the armies of the Shang dynasty, bringing the Zhou dynasty to power.

1000 BC
The Western Zhou dynasty establishes its capital at Hao.

722 BC
The Eastern Zhou dynasty begins to establish loose confederations.

221 BC
The famous Qin emperor, Shu Huangdi, comes to power.

218 – 204 BC
The Great Wall of China is built at Shu Huangdi's orders.

210 BC
Shu Huangdi dies aged 49. A huge tomb complex is built at Xianyang guarded by a life-size army of terracotta soldiers.

Aryan India & the Founding of Buddhism

1500 BC

The arrival of the Aryans in India in 1500 BC brought about the collapse of the Harappan civilization. The new people brought a new language, Sanskrit, the caste system, and an orally transmitted literature that would form the basis for Hinduism. In 563 BC, an Indian prince was born who became the Buddha and founded one of the world's great religions.

The Aryans

Around 1500 BC, pastoralists crossed the Hindu Kush into what are now India and Pakistan. These 'Aryans' or 'Indo-Europeans' had fled their homeland in Turkmenistan and Uzbekistan, possibly driven by disease or drought.

The Aryans counted their wealth in cattle and sheep and were more backward than the earlier inhabitants of the sub-continent - but they were tougher. They were warriors, beef-eaters and wine-drinkers. Their invasion seems to have been responsible for the collapse of the Harappan civilization in the Indus valley.

The Aryans settled down, adopting the way of life of the native Dravidians, but introducing some customs of their own, including the caste system. By 500 BC the Aryan language, Sanskrit, was established over the whole of the Indian sub-continent. They had no writing, passing on their history and beliefs by oral

Shiva is called the Destroyer, but with destruction he also brings regeneration.

One of many representations of Buddha, widely worshipped throughout Asia.

tradition. These traditions, called the Vedas (Books of Knowledge), were only written down much later.

The Vedas became the basis of Hinduism, one of the world's oldest surviving religions, which evolved gradually over thousands of years. Hindus worship many gods. The three main gods are Vishnu, who restores order, Brahma the creator and Shiva the destroyer. There are many sacred writings including two epic poems, the Mahabharata and the Ramayana, which tell of the gods' battles against evil.

Buddhism

Prince Siddhartha Gautama (563–483 BC) was the son of a rajah living 160 km north of Benares. Gautama was the family or clan name. At the age of 29, he left his family to live the life of an ascetic. While contemplating under a banyan tree at Gaya in Bihar he achieved enlightenment, and became known as the Buddha, or Enlightened One. He taught a religion of kindness and respect for all living creatures; before long he had many followers and Buddhism became one of the world's major religions.

The Hebrews & the Founding of Judaism

2000 BC

The Hebrews were a nomadic tribe originating in Mesopotamia, wandering through Syria, Canaan, Egypt and back to Canaan, where they finally settled, though only after a period of exile in Babylon. These tough and influential people, calling themselves first Hebrews, then Israelites, then Jews, founded a unique religion based on a single god and a set of Ten Commandments.

The origins of the Jews

The Hebrews, a tribe from southern Mesopotamia, settled in Canaan (Palestine) in about 2000 BC. Their name meant 'people from the other side' of the River Euphrates. According to the Old Testament, the first Hebrew was Abraham, a shepherd who was born in the city-state of Ur and travelled with his family to Syria and then Canaan. Abraham's grandson Jacob had 12 sons; who gave their names to the 12 Hebrew tribes.

Famine drove the Hebrews to seek refuge in Egypt, where they became slaves until their leader, Moses, led them back to Canaan.

Moses exhibits the Tables of the Law on which the Ten Commandments are inscribed.

TIME LINE	40,000BC	10,000	5000	4000	2000 BC	AD1	200	40(

The First kings of Israel

From 1020 BC onwards, the Hebrews (or Israelites as they also called themselves) prospered under three great kings, Saul, David and Solomon. Saul, who defended the Israelites against the Philistines, was anointed by Samuel as the first king of the Israelites; he was killed at the battle of Gilboa in 1012 BC. King David united the tribes of Israel into a single nation and in 994 BC made Jerusalem his capital. Solomon, who succeeded his father David in 961 BC, gained the reputation of being one of the wisest kings in history; he brought order and peace to Israel and built the first temple in Jerusalem to house the Israelites' holiest treasure, the Ark of the Covenant, a chest containing the Ten Commandments. This became the focus for their religion, which emphasized one god, Yahweh (Jehovah). After Solomon's death the kingdom was divided into Israel and Judah. The Assyrians captured Israel in 722 BC and Judah in 683 BC. The Israelites were taken into captivity in Babylon in 597 BC and released in 538 BC. From this time on the Israelites were called Jews.

The city of Jerusalem is a holy place for Jews, Muslims and Christians.

CHRONOLOGY OF EVENTS
1700 – 538 BC

1700 BC
Abraham, a prince of Ur, moves to Canaan (Palestine) and founds a new religion with only one god.

1650 BC
Captive Israelites leave Egypt to begin a migration that will eventually lead them to Canaan.

1275 BC
The Jewish religion is developed by Abraham's grandson Jacob.

1025 BC
Saul is anointed king of Hebron by the prophet Samuel.

1012 BC
Battle of Mount Gilboa. Saul and his eldest son Jonathan are killed. David becomes king of Hebron.

1005 BC
David takes Jerusalem and is anointed King of Judaea by Samuel. He makes Jerusalem his capital.

961 BC
Solomon succeeds his father David.

722 BC
The Assyrians capture Israel.

597 BC
Israelites are held captive in Babylon.

538 BC
Israelites are released from captivity, and henceforth called Jews.

The Ancient Greek City States

500 BC

Ancient Greece was made of several separate city-states, the most important being Athens and Sparta. These rival states were sometimes at war with each other, but also joined forces to fight off a Persian invasion. The Athenians developed democracy and a masterly architectural style.

City states

Classical Greece, like Mycenaean Greece, was made up of several independent city-states. The way Greece was physically laid out, with fertile basins separated by mountain ridges, naturally lent itself to this political structure. The mountains afforded protection, but the cities themselves were defended by high walls, and each city had an acropolis, a walled fortress on a hill. At the centre of the city was an agora, an open market square that also was used for public debate.

Athens and Sparta

The most important city-states were Athens and Sparta. Athens was the birthplace of democracy (government by the people) under Pericles in the sixth century BC, but it was far from our modern idea of democracy as many people, such as women and slaves, were excluded from participation in political decision-making. Athena was the guardian goddess of Athens; she was both a warrior and a judge.

Sparta was the great rival of Athens, but

they joined forces to try to fight off the Persian invasion at the battles of Thermopylae, Marathon and Salamis. In the Peloponnesian War, from 431 BC onwards, they fought one another.

In the fifth century BC, the Athenians transformed their acropolis from a fortress into a sacred precinct, with spectacular shrines and temples, including the magnificent Parthenon designed by Ictinus and Callicrates in 448 BC; it housed a colossal ivory and gold statue of Athena made by the great sculptor Pheidias. Greek architecture was perhaps the greatest ever devised. The architect Polykleitos designed a theatre at Epidaurus which seated 13,000 people; it is still there, still a functioning theatre.

The Parthenon in Athens
The name Parthenon refers to the worship of Athena Parthenos, the 'Virgin Athena' who issued fully grown from the head of her father Zeus.

600	800	1000	1200	1400	1600	1800	1900	2000

The Greek Philosophers

500 BC

The Greeks were the first people to record their questions about the world and to use reasoned arguments to explore problems. Earlier peoples wrote lists of kings and lists of offerings to gods, but the Greeks wrote full accounts of their lives. The Greeks were the first to explore, in writing, the meaning of life and the nature of the universe, which they called philosophy.

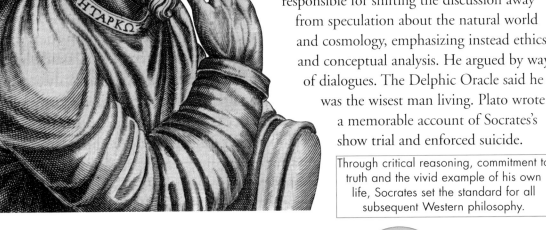

The 'New Learning' and Socrates

This 'New Learning' gained momentum in the fifth century BC, when religious considerations were left out of the arguments.

Socrates (469–399 BC) stayed in Athens all his life, wrote nothing, founded no school and had no formal following, yet with his pupil Plato and Plato's pupil Aristotle he was one of the three greatest philosophers of the ancient world. He was responsible for shifting the discussion away from speculation about the natural world and cosmology, emphasizing instead ethics and conceptual analysis. He argued by way of dialogues. The Delphic Oracle said he was the wisest man living. Plato wrote a memorable account of Socrates's show trial and enforced suicide.

Through critical reasoning, commitment to truth and the vivid example of his own life, Socrates set the standard for all subsequent Western philosophy.

TIME LINE	40,000BC	10,000	5000	4000	500 BC	AD1	200	40(

School of Athens, showing Plato and Aristotle with students.

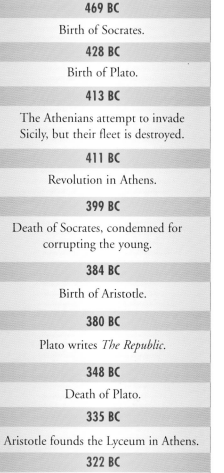

Plato (c.428–c.348 BC) was the pupil of Socrates and the teacher of Aristotle. He wrote about 30 dialogues which have had a deep effect on all subsequent thought. His *Republic* describes his utopia, a hierarchical society ruled by philosopher-kings. He also wrote a controversial description of the lost land of Atlantis.

Aristotle (384–322 BC) founded the first university, the Lyceum in Athens (335). He was what we would call a snob; he had strong class prejudices and a contempt for 'lesser breeds' and manual labour. Was it proper, he asked, for gentlemen to play musical instruments? His intellectual elitism and his interest in the absolute power of leaders like his pupil Alexander now seem depressing; in fact they must have been so at the time. After the developments of the previous 200 years, Aristotle must have seemed like a dinosaur. His writings were encyclopaedic, covering every field of knowledge, though what survives are actually lecture notes written by students and edited by Andronicus of Rhodes.

The Greek Legacy
500 BC

OVERVIEW ❖ OVERVIEW ❖ OVERVIEW ❖ OVERVIEW ❖ OVERVIEW

The Greeks wrote the first history, geography, tragedy, comedy, and launched the continuing literary tradition of Europe and North America. They valued competition, in sport and drama, and were among the first to celebrate the beauty of the human body in sculpture. Greek art has had a profound influence on all subsequent art.

History and mathematics

Herodotus was the first to write true history – and true geography. Thucydides was the first to write a detailed account of a war and its causes. Greece also produced the first mathematicians, Euclid and Pythagoras, who devised many of the rules of arithmetic and geometry that are still in use today.

Drama and games

The Greeks put a high value on drama. Many great dramas were written in the fifth century BC. Aeschylus (525–456 BC) wrote monumental tragedies such as the *Oresteia* trilogy, was born at Eleusis in 525 BC and died in 456 BC. The *Agamemnon* is thought to be the greatest ancient Greek play to have survived. Sophocles (c. 496–405 BC), the Athenian dramatist who beat Aeschylus in a drama competition in 468 BC, wrote tragedies such as *Electra, Antigone* and *Oedipus Tyrannus*. Euripides (480–406 BC) drew on archaic and disreputable myths, and drew a humanist message out of them, cleverly evading prosecution for heresy by pious conservative Athenians.

Classical Greek actors' masks depicting various expressions and emotions.

The Olympic flame is carried from Greece to the site of the Olympic Games, where it lights the main flame.

Eighteen of Euripides plays survive, more than those of Aeschylus and Sophocles put together. Greek literature, starting with Homer's *Iliad* and *Odyssey*, was the beginning of a long tradition of European and North American literature, and an inspiration to all subsequent generations of writers.

Plays were written and performed in honour of the gods. Games were organized in the same spirit. The most famous were the Olympic Games, held every 4 years at the Sanctuary of Zeus at Olympia. The pentathlon consisted of discus, long jump, javelin, wrestling and sprinting. Athletes performed naked and the perfection of the athletic male body was celebrated in many beautiful statues. Greek art has had a profound influence on all subsequent art.

Architecture
Great public buildings incorporated elaborate geometric forms and were always symmetrical. They invariably featured colonnades, rows of graceful columns supporting an elaborately corniced roof. The fluted columns were of three distinct orders – plain Doric, scrolled Ionic and leafy Corinthian. The great beauty and sophistication of this architectural style has been widely imitated in many subsequent centuries.

Ancient Rome

500 BC

The city of Rome was founded by the Etruscans and initially ruled by Etruscan kings. In 510 BC, it became a republic, ruled first by the Senate and later by a succession of emperors. By AD 100, the Roman Empire covered the whole of southern Europe and the African coast of the Mediterranean Sea.

The founding of Rome

According to Roman tradition, the city of Rome was founded in 753 BC - by the Etruscans. Early Rome, which was built for safety on seven hills, was ruled by Etruscan kings and inhabited by a mixture of Etruscans, the people who lived to the north, and Latini, who lived to the south.

In 510 BC the Etruscan rulers were driven out and Rome became a republic ruled by a Senate consisting of a group of elders. They elected two consuls each year as leaders, reserving the right to advise.

Military and economic might

Rome's greatness lay in its military strength. The Roman army consisted of full-time professional soldiers, who were paid in cash and also rewarded with rights of citizenship. The army was organized into legions of 6,000 men, each divided into ten cohorts. Each cohort consisted of 100 legionaries (foot soldiers) commanded by a centurion.

Roman foot soldiers with ornamented helmets and shields.

| TIME LINE | 40,000BC | 10,000 | 5000 | 4000 | 500 BC | AD1 | 200 | 40 |

Rome also became richer as a result of conquest, loot and slavery. Conquest produced dangerously ambitious generals, like Julius Caesar, who used their military success as a springboard to political power. Caesar succeeded in having himself declared dictator for life and this alarmed many of the senators, who plotted his assassination in 44 BC.

Emperors

A power struggle followed. Caesar's nephew Augustus was in effect an emperor, though he cleverly insisted he was merely princeps, first citizen.

The succession of emperors, including Claudius, Caligula, Nero, Hadrian and Trajan, depended less on family than on ability. The Roman Empire itself grew until by AD 100 it was huge, stretching from Britain to Syria and Egypt.

Above: Map of the Roman Empire, in red, at its peak.
Right: Gaius Julius Caesar, Roman Emperor.

CHRONOLOGY OF EVENTS
735 BC – AD 100

753 BC

The city of Rome is founded according to Roman tradition.

510 BC

Etruscan rulers of Rome are driven out. The city of Rome becomes a republic.

60 BC

Julius Caesar forms ruling triumvirate with Pompey and Crassus.

44 BC

Julius Caesar is assassinated.

27 BC

Octavian founds the Roman Empire, adopting the name Augustus Caesar.

AD 40

Caligula is assassinated and Claudius becomes emperor.

AD 54

Claudius dies, poisoned on the orders of the Empress Agrippina, who hopes to rule through her son Nero.

AD 100

Roman Empire covers all southern Europe.

The Roman Legacy

200 BC

The Romans kept alive and passed on the great architectural tradition of ancient Greece, adding the use of concrete and huge domes in 200 BC. They also established a European road system of which much is still in use, and high standards of domestic architecture, introducing central heating and plumbed toilets. The idea of a pseudo-benevolent 'Roman Peace' was revived in the nineteenth century AD to justify the British Empire.

The Romans built straight roads, not only to facilitate rapid marching over long distances, but also to enable them to see clearly in both directions, thereby reducing the risk of surprise attack.

Roads

The Romans made a continent-wide network of roads connecting their cities, wherever possible by straight-line routes. Stout arched bridges were used to cross valleys. The intention was to make the rapid movement of troops possible. Many of these roads are still in use, many times rebuilt and covered with tarmac, to serve modern commercial needs.

TIME LINE	40,000BC	10,000	5000	4000	200 BC	AD1	200	400

The Colosseum is one of the finest examples of Roman architecture and engineering. Built as an arena for a variety of public spectacles, it could seat over 50,000 spectators.

CHRONOLOGY OF EVENTS
220 BC – AD 312

220 BC

The Flaminian Way, the road between Rome and Rimini, is completed.

200 BC

The first huge domes are built.

120 BC

Temple of Concord is built in Rome (first large-scale use of concrete).

51 BC

Julius Caesar writes *On the Gallic War.*

AD 50

The Acqua Claudia, an aqueduct from Campagna to Rome, is built.

AD 71

The Arch of Titus is built.

AD 80

The Colosseum is built at the orders of the Emperor Titus.

AD 114

Trajan's Column is built in Rome.

AD 120

Hadrian's Wall is built in Britain.

AD 312

The Arch of Constantine is built in Rome.

Buildings

Some magnificent public buildings were created, often borrowing their style from classical Greece. Usually cities were laid out like Roman military camps, within a systematic grid plan, which has been copied by many later cultures, from Anglo-Saxon England to nineteenth century America. Stone and brick were in common use in ancient Rome. From 200 BC concrete was used as well, at first for foundations, but then also for making huge domed roofs. Round arches and their extension, barrel vaults, were favoured; the Colosseum is a maze of barrel-vaulted passageways. These features were the basis of Norman or Romanesque architecture hundreds of years later.

Roman domestic architecture also set ambitious standards, with five-storey apartment blocks. Homes were carefully decorated with wall paintings and centrally heated. Plumbing for toilets was regarded as essential.

Pax Romana

Roman conquest and rule could be brutal, but the authority imposed was absolute and put an end to small local wars, allowing people to farm and trade in peace. This Pax Romana (Roman Peace) was the model and justification for the British Empire with its Pax Britannica.

Jesus of Nazareth & the Founding of Christianity

7 BC

OVERVIEW ❖ OVERVIEW ❖ OVERVIEW ❖ OVERVIEW ❖ OVERVIEW

Jesus was a first century Jewish religious teacher and healer. His followers believed he was the long-awaited Messiah, who would save the Jewish people from Roman oppression, but Jesus was interested only in saving people's souls in preparation for the expected end of the world. After his execution for trouble-making in Jerusalem, his followers spread his teachings through the Roman world.

The Messiah

For several centuries the Jews had lived in expectation that a saviour, the Messiah, would appear to lead and rescue them. When Jesus of Nazareth grew up and took up his role as a religious teacher, Judaea was under Roman rule. It was understandable that some of his followers, who believed that he was the Messiah or the Christ (the anointed one), assumed

Jesus's last supper with his disciples, painting by Leonardo da Vinci.

TIME LINE	40,000BC	10,000	5000	4000	500	7 BC	200	40(

that he would lead a revolt against the Romans, but Jesus refused to do this.

Jesus's life and death

Jesus was probably born in Nazareth in about 7 BC. When he grew up he probably became a carpenter like his father. In about AD 27 he began his public career as a religious healer, teaching in vivid parables. He spoke about the coming of the kingdom of God, and evidently expected the existing order to pass away at any moment. As a result of his criticism of the religious authorities and the disturbances he caused in Jerusalem, Jesus fell foul of both the religious leaders and the Roman authorities. The Romans arrested him on the eve of a major religious festival in AD 33 and after a summary trial put him to death by crucifixion.

The spread of Christianity

The teachings of Jesus were spread by his followers, especially Paul, who took what became a new religion outside the Jewish world.

They said that even non-Jews could become Christians. In AD 250 the persecution of Christians began, as their loyalties were not first and foremost to the Emperor or to Rome. The Emperor Constantine made Christianity legal in AD 313, and by 400 it was the official religion of the Roman Empire.

CHRONOLOGY OF EVENTS
7 BC – AD 400

7 BC

Jesus is born, probably at Nazareth.

4 BC

Herod the Great, King of Judaea, dies.

AD 27

Jesus begins his public career as a religious healer and teacher.

AD 33

At about this date Jesus travels from Galilee to Jerusalem with his followers to observe the Passover. The Roman procurator Pontius Pilate has Jesus crucified for sedition.

AD 63

A fire destroys half the city of Rome. Christians are blamed for starting it. Paul is probably crucified in the aftermath.

AD 250

The large-scale persecution of Christians begins under the Emperor Decius.

AD 301

The King of Armenia makes Christianity his official religion, the first head of state to do so.

AD 313

Emperor Constantine makes Christianity legal.

AD 400

Christianity becomes the official religion of the Roman Empire.

THE
MIDDLE AGES

The Barbarians
& The Fall of Rome
200 AD

The Roman Empire's long decline began when a series of emperors followed each other in quick succession, weakening Rome's power to act. This encouraged native peoples on the fringes of the Empire to attack. The Emperor Diocletian's response, to divide the Empire in two, merely weakened it further. It was finally destroyed by massive attacks on Rome itself by Visigoths and Vandals in 410 and 455.

Internal collapse

Rome began to decline in the third century. Emperors followed one another in rapid succession, either removed by the army or assassinated in dynastic power struggles, and this weakened Rome's ability to hold the Empire together. The Emperor Diocletian decided in 286 that the Empire could not be ruled by one man alone and divided it in two, appointing a co-emperor, Maximian, to rule the Western Empire. A few years later he experimentally divided the Empire in four,

The Fall of Rome – Alaric's Visigoths ride exuberantly into Rome.

and Constantius Chlorus and Galerius were proclaimed Caesars. After Diocletian's abdication in 305, his successor, Constantine, made Byzantium on the Black Sea his capital, calling it Constantinople; this intensified the division between the two empires, the East becoming grander, the West becoming weaker still.

Attacks from outside

Sensing the lack of contral, many tribal groups on the northern fringes of the Empire went on the offensive. Vandals, Huns, Goths (Ostrogoths and Visigoths) invaded from the north-east, Franks and Saxons from the north. Rome was sacked by a Visigoth horde led by Alaric (c.370–410) in 410, which sent shock waves throughout Europe; Rome was sacked a second time in 455 by a Vandal army, which brought about the collapse of the West. The last emperor of the West was deposed in 476.

The Eastern Empire lasted longer. Justinian succeeded in reconquering territories which the barbarians had invaded in Spain, Africa and Italy, and tried to re-establish the old Roman Empire, but the regained land was soon lost again.

arbares: J. Che..

Barbarians

The so-called 'Barbarians' were in many ways as civilized as the Romans, though less concerned with central control. Many of them cultivated Roman ways, adopted Roman names and even Roman titles; some even intermarried with Roman aristocrats. Stilicho (c.365–408), who was a great general in command of the Western Roman army from 393 until 408, was half-Roman, half-Vandal. The main difference was the lack of literacy.

CHRONOLOGY OF EVENTS
AD 284 – 476

284

The new Roman Emperor Diocletian decides that the Empire cannot be ruled by one man alone and divides it in two.

305

Diocletian abdicates at the age of 60.

405

The Colosseum is closed, a sign that Rome is shutting down.

410

Rome is sacked by Visigoth horde led by Alaric.

455

The Empire is destroyed by a massive attack on Rome by Vandals. From now on Germanic 'barbarians' manage the Empire.

475

Roman commander Orestes expels the Emperor Julius Nepos and names his own son, Augustulus, Emperor of the West.

476

The Western Empire founded by Augustus is formally ended at Ravenna. The last emperor of the West, Augustulus, is deposed by the Saxon leader Odovacar. The boy is treated kindly and sent to Naples to live on a large pension.

Ancient Japan

AD 200

OVERVIEW ❖ OVERVIEW ❖ OVERVIEW ❖ OVERVIEW ❖ OVERVIEW

Japan has existed as a state since AD 167, when about 30 states joined together under the priestess Himiko. China, then a more advanced civilization, had a strong influence over Japan at that time. Subsequent centuries were dominated by a succession of powerful families including the Yamato and the Fujiwara. A thousand years ago, Japan was dominated by the Shinto religion, a variant of Buddhism.

Japanese masks are impressive works of art produced by skilled craftsmen.

Early Japan and the Yamato period

People have been living in Japan continuously since 30,000 BC. Around 250 BC, the Yayoi tribe became the most influential in Japan. They used bronze and iron, probably brought in from Korea. In AD 167 about 30 small independent states joined together and a priestess called Himiko became their ruler. Himiko sent ambassadors to seek the support and friendship of the Chinese. The Chinese civilization was well established and became very influential in Japan over the next few centuries.

From the fourth century, Japan was ruled by an emperor. By 646 much of Japan was ruled by emperors belonging to the Yamato tribe. Later emperors, right down to the present, have claimed descent from the Yamato emperors, who in turn claimed descent from the Sun goddess.

Fujiwara period

In the ninth century, the Fujiwara family became very powerful when Fujiwara Yoshifusa's daughter married the emperor. On the emperor's death in 858, their son became emperor and Fujiwara became the first regent from outside the royal family; this marked the

TIME LINE | **40,000BC** | **10,000** | **5000** | **4000** | **500** | **AD 1** | **AD 200** | 40

beginning of the Fujiwara period. More Fujiwara girls were married to emperors and it became the custom to appoint a Fujiwara regent, who became the actual ruler, while the emperor spent his time on religious matters. During the Fujiwara period, which lasted into the eleventh century, art and literature flourished. Ladies at court wrote books that are still read in Japan today. Kyoto, the capital, suffered many fires and earthquakes; it was thought they were caused by the spirits of officials banished by the Fujiwaras. Shrines were built to pacify the spirits.

Shinto religion

Most Japanese people belonged to the Shinto religion, a religion that was strongly influenced by Buddhism. Buddhist ceremonies were used for funerals and other occasions. Clay figures of ferocious armoured warriors were used to protect temples and shrines from demons.

CHRONOLOGY OF EVENTS
2200 BC – AD 1192

2200 BC

The Jomon culture flourishes in Japan.

200 BC

The Yamato tribe dominate Japan.

AD 167

About 30 separate states join together under the priestess Himiko.

AD 390

The Japanese conquer Korea.

AD 646

Much of Japan is ruled by emperors belonging to the Yamato tribe.

AD 858

The Fujiwara clan become the ruling elite.

AD 1192

The ruthless general Minamoto Yoritomo leads the Minamoto clan to power. From this time, until 1868, the shoguns (generals) rule Japan as military dictators.

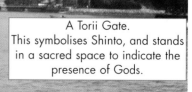

A Torii Gate.
This symbolises Shinto, and stands in a sacred space to indicate the presence of Gods.

Polynesia

AD 300

OVERVIEW ❖ OVERVIEW ❖ OVERVIEW ❖ OVERVIEW ❖ OVERVIEW

The Polynesians colonized a huge region, comprising the islands of the central and western Pacific Ocean, which had never been inhabited before. They set off on this venture from New Guinea in 1600 BC and reached the middle of the Pacific by AD 300.

Great colonists and navigators

The Polynesians originally came from Eastern Asia, colonizing New Guinea. From 1600 BC onwards, they started island-hopping through the islands to the east (Melanesia), from New Britain to the New Hebrides, Fiji and Tonga, taking with them their chickens, pigs, coconuts, yams, breadfruit and bananas. The trail of incised Lapita pottery, which has been radiocarbon dated, records their rapid movement eastwards, reaching Samoa and Tonga by 1000 BC, and their colonization of a vast and previously uninhabited region.

Later, they ventured out into the middle of the Pacific, settling Tahiti in AD 500, and spreading out from there to Easter Island, then Hawaii in 600 and New Zealand in 800.

Although in 1947 Thor Heyerdahl proved that it was possible to sail westwards from Peru

Catamaran of a type widely used, with local variations, throughout Polynesia.

TIME LINE	40,000BC	10,000	5000	4000	500	AD1	2	AD 300

to Tuamotu Island, archaeologists have conclusively proved that that the Polynesians' migration route was from the other side of the Pacific.

The Polynesians were master navigators. They learnt how to identify the distinctive banner clouds that develop over each island group, and betray their location even when the islands themselves are invisible beyond the horizon. They also devised star maps woven out of natural fibres to help them navigate at night. They were able to find their way across empty expanses of ocean in their outrigger canoes.

Easter Island statues

It was on Easter Island that the Polynesians created their most remarkable artwork, some huge stone heads up to 12 metres high and weighing up to 50 tonnes. They stand in rows near the shore, looking enigmatically out to sea. Some of them still wear 'topknots' of red stone. They were carved and dragged into position between AD 1000 and 1600 and held some religious significance, now long forgotten.

The Easter Island Statues.

CHRONOLOGY OF EVENTS
1600 BC – AD 1600

1600 BC

The Polynesians venture eastwards from New Guinea in open canoes.

1000 BC

They reach Samoa and Tonga.

AD 300

The Polynesians reach the middle of the Pacific.

AD 400

The Polynesians reach Easter Island.

AD 500

The Polynesians settle in Tahiti.

AD 600

They reach Hawaii.

AD 800

They reach New Zealand, settling mainly on the North Island as 'Maoris'.

AD 1000–1600

Polynesian colonists carve and raise the huge stone heads on Easter Island.

Byzantium
400 AD

OVERVIEW ❖ OVERVIEW ❖ OVERVIEW ❖ OVERVIEW ❖ OVERVIEW

When the Western Roman Empire fell in the fifth century, the power vacuum was filled by the Eastern Empire, which became known as the Byzantine Empire. Although after 565 it had little in the way of territory, the Byzantine Empire grew rich from trade. It also became a focus of culture and learning and the seat of a dynamic Christian church, the Orthodox Church.

Justinian and Theodora

St Sophia, the Church of Holy Wisdom, built by order of Justinian between 532 and 537 BC.

The old Eastern Roman Empire had Constantinople as its capital. It was built on the site of the even older Greek port of Byzantium. When the Western Empire finally collapsed in 476, Constantinople became the capital of what came to be called the Byzantine Empire.

Under the Emperor Justinian I (ruled 527–565), a huge area was reconquered: southern Spain, Italy and North Africa. Justinian was ably supported by his co-ruler and wife, a

TIME LINE	40,000BC	10,000	5000	4000	500	AD1	AD 400

Byzantium Coins

former actress and great beauty, the Empress Theodora. By 565, Justinian and his great general Belisarius had brilliantly expanded the new empire to include the whole of the eastern Mediterranean as well.

A trading empire

After Justinian died, a lot of this land was lost again, but Constantinople remained a key trading centre. It had a marvellous location, where a major sea route from the Black Sea to the Mediterranean crossed a major land route from Europe to Asia. Like the earlier Minoan 'empire', it did not depend on ownership of huge territories but on a good location and on trading contacts.

The Byzantine Empire produced grain, olives, wine, silk and gold, and traded these for ivory, spices, furs and precious stones from Africa and the Far East.

A cultural centre

Constantinople was a great cultural centre, a centre of learning. It also developed its own brand of Christianity in the form of the Orthodox Church. Such was the Byzantine Empire's supremacy that for several centuries St Sophia, with its huge dome, was the greatest church in Christendom. St Sophia, or the Church of Holy Wisdom, was built on Justinian's orders between 532 and 537, and used a workforce of 10,000.

Spices and wine were among the goods traded between Byzantium and Africa and the Far East.

CHRONOLOGY OF EVENTS
AD 476 – 578

476

The Western Roman Empire falls. Constantinople becomes the capital of the new Byzantine Empire.

527

Justinus I, Emperor of the East, adopts his nephew Justinian as co-emperor. Justinus dies and Justinian becomes sole emperor.

537

St Sophia, Constantinople, is completed at Justinian's orders.

541

Justinian prepares plans to conquer Gaul and Britain, but abandons them when he contracts plague. The Great Plague of Justinian sweeps across Europe.

565

By the end of his reign, Justinian and his great general Belisarius have expanded the new empire to include the entire eastern Mediterranean as well. Justinian dies.

578

The Emperor Justin II dies insane, succeeded by his general Tiberius as Tiberius II Constantius.

The Prophet Mohammed & the Founding of Islam
570 BC

OVERVIEW ❖ OVERVIEW ❖ OVERVIEW ❖ OVERVIEW ❖ OVERVIEW

Mohammed (570–632) founded a new religion, based in part on Judaeo-Christian monotheism and in part on a regime of regular prayer and the avoidance of forbidden foods and drinks. Fired with enthusiasm for Islam, the Arab world turned into an Empire rivalling those around it.

The Prophet Mohammed

Mohammed was born in Mecca in 570, the nephew of the chief of a small tribe. Then he worked for a wealthy widow, Khadija, whom he later married. They had six children. When he was about 40, in c.610, he had a vision in which the Archangel Gabriel told him to preach that there was one god, called Allah, and he began preaching in Mecca. After his life was threatened, he fled to Medina; his migration in 622, known as the Hegira, marks the start of the Muslim calendar.

Mohammed's teachings

In Mohammed's day, the Arab peoples worshipped many gods. Mohammed's beliefs were strongly influenced by the Jewish-Christian belief in one god and it was his monotheism that put him in danger. In Medina, Mohammed and his

A page from the holy Koran, beautifully decorated in intricate detail.

TIME LINE	40,000BC	10,000	5000	4000	500	AD1	200	40

The Dome of the Rock, in Jerusalem, is a sacred site and place of worship for Muslims.

followers organized the first Muslim state and built the first mosque. He taught that everyone could be saved by praying regularly and eating only prescribed foods and drinks. These teachings, together with Mohammed's prophecies, were written down in the holy book of Islam, the Koran.

The spread of Islam

Mohammed's following grew fast. Poor Arabs in Medina saw in his teachings the prospect of a fairer society. In 630, Mohammed returned to Mecca and became its ruler, banning the worship of idols and excluding unbelievers - who are still not allowed into the city. The Islamic empire quickly spread across Arabia. After Mohammed's death in 632, his new religion spread east to India and west into Europe. Mohammed was succeeded as Islamic leader by his wife Aishah's father, Abu Bakr, the first caliph.

In 634 and 636 the Arabs, emboldened by the belief that death in battle took them straight to paradise, had defeated the Byzantine army and went on conquer Persia by 643. The Islamic Empire stretched from Pakistan to Spain at its greatest extent and was only halted when a Frankish army defeated Arabs and Berbers from Morocco at Poitiers in 732.

Anglo-Saxon Colonization

AD 500

OVERVIEW ❖ OVERVIEW ❖ OVERVIEW ❖ OVERVIEW ❖ OVERVIEW

Germanic tribes crossed the North Sea and colonized eastern England in the fifth and sixth centuries. They were opposed by the Britons; the two sides organized themselves under commanders-in-chief. The seven Anglo-Saxon kingdoms eventually became one – England – in 954.

The 'invasion'

When Roman troops left Britain undefended in the fifth century AD, Germanic invaders began to colonize England. The Jutes colonized Kent, the Angles settled the east coast from East Anglia to Northumberland, and the Saxons colonized Sussex, Hampshire, Dorset and Wiltshire. The incomers gradually spread westward.

England was divided into seven Anglo-Saxon kingdoms, Wessex (West Saxons), Sussex (South Saxons), Essex (East Saxons), Kent, East Anglia, Mercia and Northumbria.

British opposition

The local British communities put up intermittent resistance, led by an overking or dux bellorum. Early texts name Arthur as dux bellorum in the early sixth century. Arthur's great victory at the Battle of Mount Badon (Bath) halted the Anglo-Saxon colonization for a couple of decades. The Anglo-Saxons in turn organized their armies under a commander-in-chief they called the bretwalda, Lord of Britain. The first bretwalda was Aelle, King of Sussex, who may have been Arthur's opposite number on the battlefield.

People

For a long time it was assumed the British were wiped out as the Anglo-Saxons advanced, but various studies (DNA and bone structure) show that it was mainly the aristocracy that was replaced; the ordinary people were left alone.

TIME LINE	40,000BC	10,000	5000	4000	500	AD1	200	400

A fierce hand-to-hand battle between Alfred's men and the Vikings.

CHRONOLOGY OF EVENTS
AD 440 – 954

440

Roman troops are withdrawn from Britain to defend Rome.

441

Saxon settlers establish a colony in Essex.

449

England is colonized piecemeal from now on by Angles, Jutes and Saxons.

516

Battle of Mount Badon. Arthur's great victory at Bath halted the Anglo-Saxon advance.

537

Battle of Camlann: defeat of the Britons under Arthur.

789

Viking raids and invasions begin.

878

The Viking threat is overcome by King Alfred.

954

The seven Anglo-Saxon kingdoms become one – England.

Place names

In eastern England, most of the names of settlements and landmarks were replaced with Germanic names. Anglo-Saxon place-names can often be recognized by their endings: -ing, -ham, -ton, -fold, -den and -hurst.

The Viking challenge

Before the Anglo-Saxon colonization could be completed, it was challenged by the Vikings. From 789 onwards there were Viking raids and invasions. It was only in 878 that the Viking threat was overcome by King Alfred and an Anglo-Saxon kingdom could be created. That happened in 954 and since then England has never been divided.

Charlemagne & the Christian Mission in Europe

AD 771

When the Western Roman Empire fell, the power vacuum in France and Germany was filled by the Franks, whose charismatic Christian emperor, Charlemagne built a new 'Holy Roman Empire'. The enterprise was greatly helped by the work of missionaries and monks.

Clovis, Charlemagne and the Franks

The power vacuum left by the fall of the Western Roman Empire was first filled (in France) by the Franks. The Merovingian dynasty, initiated by Clovis (465-511), was overthrown in 751 by Pippin the Short (c.715-768), who founded the Carolingian dynasty. On Pippin's death in 768, his sons Carloman (751-771) and Charles (747-814) inherited the Frankish kingdom. When Carloman died in 771, Charles became sole ruler. He was a great military leader, expanding the kingdom to include the whole of France, Benelux, Germany and part of northern Italy, making it the most powerful kingdom in Europe.

Charles became known as Charles the Great, Charlemagne. He supported the Pope and extended the power of the Christian church in his kingdom. In return, on Christmas Day 800 Pope Leo III crowned Charlemagne Holy Roman Emperor.

Charlemagne, King of the Franks and Holy Roman Emperor.

TIME LINE	40,000BC	10,000	5000	4000	500	AD1	200	4C

Charlemagne encouraged scholarship within the monasteries and abbeys. The palace school in his capital, Aachen, was the main centre of learning in the West.

Winfrith and other missionaries

Much of the Carolingian achievement was made possible by the activities of Christian missionaries and diplomats. The monasteries were havens of security in an uncertain world. They provided accommodation for travellers. They were centres of learning. It was the monks who wrote the history. Bede (c.673–735), based in north-east England, wrote The Ecclesiastical History of the English People (731). A key figure was Winfrith, later St Boniface (c.680–754), who converted 100,000 Germans to Christianity. He met and corresponded with a startling range of people – priests, bishops, archbishops, kings and a succession of popes. Winfrith used his huge influence to weld central Europe into a well-administrated region under the rule of Christian princes. He organized the coronation of Pippin, and so prepared the way for Charlemagne. Winfrith was eventually murdered by robbers in what is now northern Holland. He was later given the accolade of 'the greatest Englishman'.

The throne of Charlemagne at Aachen Cathedral in Germany.

CHRONOLOGY OF EVENTS
AD 747 – 814

747

Charlemagne is born, eldest son of Pippin the Short.

768

Pippin dies, succeeded by his sons Carloman and Charlemagne.

771

Carloman dies and Charlemagne becomes sole ruler of the Franks. Charlemagne wages war on the Saxons.

774

Charlemagne visits Rome.

782

Charlemagne makes Saxony a Frankish province.

800

Pope Leo III crowned Charlemagne Holy Roman Emperor.

814

Charlemagne dies of pleurisy aged 71, succeeded by his son Louis I.

Viking Expansion

AD 800

From 800 onwards the Vikings began migrating by sea from Scandinavia to France, Britain and Russia. They looted monasteries and towns, but they also developed widespread trading operations with Russia and the East.

Migrants, colonists and traders

The Vikings began to migrate from their Scandinavian homelands around AD 800. In fast shallow-draft sailing-ships (longships) they were able to cross open sea and sail up rivers such as the Rhine, Seine and Loire, looting monasteries and towns. They settled in Normandy, which in 911 was handed over to the Viking leader, Rollo, by the king of France. Vikings settled in eastern England, where their settlements can be recognized by their

A Viking longship.

TIME LINE	40,000BC	10,000	5000	4000	500	AD1	200	40

names, which often end in –by and –thorpe, and in northern Scotland. In 1013 King Sven (Sweyn Forkbeard) of Denmark became king of England. His son Cnut (Canute) became king of England (1016–1042) and headed a huge Viking Empire that included Denmark, Sweden, Norway and Iceland.

The Vikings used Iceland as a penal colony, sending their criminals there; some went on from there to form a short-lived colony in Greenland. It is possible that Viking Greenlanders went on to explore and possibly settle in North America, though the Vinland Map, which gives evidence of this, is now believed to be a forgery.

Swedish Vikings sailed east across the Baltic Sea in 850 and began trading with the Russians, setting up trading posts at Novgorod and Kiev They reached the Black Sea and the cities of Constantinople and Baghdad using sturdy square-sailed ships called knarrs. Together with the Arabs, the Vikings were the greatest traders of their time (800–1100).

Culture and religion

Viking culture hinged on the romance of adventure, which supplemented agricultural production at home with loot acquired by piracy abroad. They wrote in stick-like characters called runes. The Vikings had many gods. The days of the week are named after them: Tiw's Day, Woden's Day, Thor's Day, Frigg's Day. They believed in a warrior heaven called Valhalla.

CHRONOLOGY OF EVENTS
AD 800 – 1016

800

Vikings begin migrating by sea from Scandinavia.

850

Swedish Vikings sail east across the Baltic Sea and begin trading with the Russians. Rurik makes himself King of Kiev.

862

King Rurik founds Novgorod, makes himself Grand Prince and establishes what will become the Russian royal family.

865

The Russian Vikings sack Constantinople.

911

The king of France hands Normandy over to the Viking leader, Rollo.

1013

King Sven of Denmark becomes king of England.

1016

Sven's son Cnut (Canute) becomes king of England and heads a huge Viking Empire that includes Denmark, Sweden, Norway and Iceland.

Aztecs & Incas

AD 1500

OVERVIEW ❖ OVERVIEW ❖ OVERVIEW ❖ OVERVIEW ❖ OVERVIEW

In 1500 two great native empires were well-established in the New World: the Aztec in central America and the Inca in South America. The Aztec brutally sacrificed thousands of captives in the capital, Tenochtitlan. The Inca empire is remembered for its gold, and for the ease with which a very small number of Spanish adventurers conquered it.

Tenochtitlan and the Aztecs

By 1500 the Aztecs had created a large empire in central America. The Aztec capital, Tenochtitlan, was a vast city built on an island in a lake. To feed all the inhabitants, food was produced on artificial islands or chinampas. Conquered people were required to bring food as tribute; they also brought raw materials such as gold, silver and jade.

Aztec culture

This warrior culture reached its peak in the sixteenth century. All young men had to do 5 years' military service, starting at the age of 17. Some stayed in the army because it was possible for anyone with ability to rise through the ranks. One function of the Aztec army was to capture prisoners and take them back to Tenochtitlan for sacrifice.

The Aztecs worshipped gods of sun, war, wind and rain. All these required human sacrifices, which took place on the summits of huge pyramids at the centre of Tenochtitlan. The victims had their hearts ripped out by priests with stone knives.

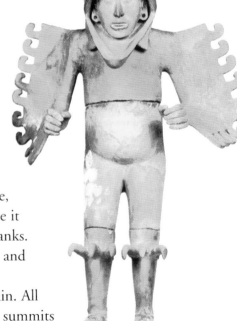

Representation of an eagle knight, one of the highest military orders.

TIME LINE	40,000BC	10,000	5000	4000	500	AD1	200	40

Machu Picchu, an Inca stronghold in a remote setting, remained undiscovered by the Spanish adventurers.

The Aztec legacy

On their chinampas, the Aztecs grew avocados, limes and tomatoes, foods that were unknown in Europe until European explorers made contact in the sixteenth century.

The Inca Empire

The Inca empire developed in South America, covering what is now Peru and northern Chile and reaching a peak in about 1500. When the ruler Huayna Capac died in 1525, the Inca empire was divided between his sons, Huascar ruling the south from Cuzco, Atahualpa ruling the north. This led to civil war, which the invading Spanish conquistadors were able to exploit. A relatively small force of Spaniards, led by Francisco Pizarro, was able to take over the Inca empire. Atahualpa himself was imprisoned by Pizarro and treacherously strangled. The Incas were farmers, craftsmen and master builders. The ruins of one of their magnificent hill towns, Machu Picchu, still stand high in the Andes.

CHRONOLOGY OF EVENTS
AD 1480 – 1531

1480

The last Aztec emperor, Montezuma II, is born.

1500

Inca and Aztec Empires reach their peak.

1502

Montezuma II ascends to the throne of the Aztec Empire at Tenochtitlan.

1519

Cortez sets sail from Cuba to conquer New Spain (Mexico).
Cortez captures Montezuma.

1520

Aztecs drive Cortez out of Mexico.

1521

Cortez takes the great city of Tenochtitlan after an 85-day battle. Montezuma is killed in the fighting.

1525

The Inca ruler Huayna Capac dies at Quito. The empire is divided between his sons, Huascar and Atahualpa.

1531

Atahualpa has his brother put to death. Pizarro conquers the Inca Empire and has King Atahualpa strangled.

Peasants' Revolts:
Rebellion & Repression
AD 1300

OVERVIEW ❖ OVERVIEW ❖ OVERVIEW ❖ OVERVIEW ❖ OVERVIEW

In the fourteenth century farm workers in Europe were poor and badly treated. They rebelled against their landowners and kings – but to no avail. The rebellions were stamped out with great brutality.

Fourteenth century rebellions

Immediately after the Black Death of 1347–9 there was a shortage of workers in Europe and farm labourers were better paid as a result. But wars, such as England's Hundred Years' War with France, resulted in an increase in taxation. Increasing poverty resulted in three rebellions in the fourteenth century.

The first revolt was in Flanders (Belgium) in 1323–28, when Peasants and farmers refused to pay taxes. The conflict between peasants and landlords led to civil war, and only the intervention of the French army crushed the rebellion.

Wat Tyler leads the people in the Peasant's Revolt.

TIME LINE	40,000BC	10,000	5000	4000	500	AD1	200	40

The second revolt broke out in northern France in 1358, this time against the hordes of mercenaries who were ravaging the countryside. It was known as the Jacquerie, after the term of contempt used for French peasants, Jacques Bonhomme – Goodman Jack. The French authorities put the rebellion down with great ferocity, killing 20,000 peasants.

Poll Tax and the Peasants' Revolt

The third revolt broke out in England, this time provoked by a poll tax. The shilling tax was a week's wages, which the peasants could not afford. Farm workers from every county in south-east England joined in the 'Peasants' Revolt' of 1381, led by Wat Tyler, who was probably a tiler from Essex and a priest called John Ball. Farm workers from Essex and Kent took Rochester Castle, moved to Canterbury and then marched on London, where 60,000 of them assembled at Blackheath.

Tyler was met by the 14 year old King Richard II and the Mayor of London, William Walworth, at Smithfield. The King made promises which he later did not honour, and the rebels were persuaded to disperse. The rebellion was not a complete failure, in that it showed that the working class would not accept injustice indefinitely.

John Ball was in Maidstone Gaol when the Peasants' Revolt broke out, and the peasants freed him, intending to make him Archbishop of Canterbury. At Blackheath he preached memorably, 'When Adam delved and Eve span, who was then a gentleman?'. After the rebellion, he was hanged for treason.

Wat Tyler was stabbed by Walworth during the confrontation with the King. When Walworth later discovered that Tyler had been removed to St Bartholomew's Hospital, he had Tyler dragged out and beheaded.

CHRONOLOGY OF EVENTS
AD 1323 – 1450

1323

First peasants' revolt breaks out in Flanders.

1358

The Jacquerie, a second peasants' revolt, breaks out in northern France.

1359

In Bruges revolutionaries wearing red hats try to overturn the government.

1380

John Wycliffe translates the Bible into English, which is seen as a subversive act.

1381

Peasants' Revolt against the poll tax in south-east England, led by Wat Tyler and a priest called John Ball. Tyler is murdered.

1450

Jack Cade's Rebellion. Cade raises a peasant army of 40,000 in Kent and marches on London. The rebellion disintegrates and disperses. Cade is hunted down and killed in Heathfield in Sussex.

Gothic Art & Architecture
AD 1200

OVERVIEW ❖ OVERVIEW ❖ OVERVIEW ❖ OVERVIEW ❖ OVERVIEW

The Gothic style (1200–1500) broke away from Roman-influenced (Romanesque) architecture, replacing round with pointed arches and vaults. Churches and cathedrals became taller and lighter. They embodied and contained most of the art work that ordinary people saw.

Church architecture.

The Romanesque style of architecture as developed in Europe in the ninth–eleventh centuries was a heavy, plain and simple style drawing strongly on Roman architecture. In particular it featured round arches, round pillars and semicircular barrel vaults.

The Gothic style of architecture replaced round arches with pointed arches, and taller, slenderer, more graceful columns. Churches and cathedrals became taller, lighter, often conveying an impression of weightlessness. The Early English style began in 1200.

A hundred years later, the Decorated style came in and a third phase, Perpendicular, started in about 1370. This final phase featured much larger windows, often using plain glass, making the churches much lighter than ever before.

Churches and cathedrals were by far the biggest

Wells Cathedral in Somerset was the first major English cathedral to be built entirely in the Gothic style.

TIME LINE	40,000BC	10,000	5000	4000	500	AD1	200	4(

and most substantial structures in most communities, soaring above the one- and two-storey wooden houses of the poor. The great buildings also involved huge teams of workers, including both unskilled labourers and highly skilled craftsmen, often for several generations. They were major community projects and expressions of community identity.

Church art

Medieval church interiors had no pews or chairs. People stood throughout services, though there were

ledges for the old and sick to lean on. The windows were often richly decorated with stained glass. The walls were richly decorated with paintings of scenes from the Bible. A favourite subject was the Last Judgement, often painted over the chancel arch. Even the pillars and the exteriors of cathedrals were brightly painted. Church art was important community art; everybody saw it, and many saw no other kind of art.

Paintings, often on wood panels, were frequently of religious subjects. Some aristocrats and merchants commissioned portraits. A few scenes of everyday life and landscapes were painted.

CHRONOLOGY OF EVENTS
AD 800 – 1540

800–1200
The Romanesque style of architecture develops in Europe.

1163
Work begins on the Gothic cathedral of Notre Dame in Paris.

1200
Early English style begins in Britain.

1225
Rheims cathedral (begun).

1258
Salisbury cathedral.

1300
Decorated style begins.

1370
Perpendicular style begins.

1420
Brunelleschi begins work on Florence cathedral.

1540
Perpendicular style ends in Britain.

Khmer Empire & Angkor Wat

AD 800

OVERVIEW ❖ OVERVIEW ❖ OVERVIEW ❖ OVERVIEW ❖ OVERVIEW

The Khmer empire (c.800–1500) developed as the Khmer people united and extended their territory by conquest. They built a capital city, Angkor Thom, with a spectacular temple called Angkor Wat. Its impressive ruins can still be seen.

The Khmer empire

In 802, in what is now Cambodia, the Khmer people were unified by King Jayavarman I to make the Khmer empire. They were a warlike people, conquering the surrounding lands in the course of many battles, using 200,000 war elephants.

The Khmers wrote books on a variety of materials – vellum, palm leaves and paper – but they have long since vanished through fire, termites and decay. Even so, a great deal can be learnt about them from contemporary Chinese histories. The Khmers also left carvings in the substantial remains of their spectacular buildings at Angkor Thom (the Great City) and Angkor Wat (its Great Temple).

Khmer way of life

The Khmers were farmers and fishermen, many of them living in houses on stilts round the shores of Lake Tonle Sap, as Cambodians still do today. Rice was their main food, and

A Cambodian monk, pausing to rest against one of the columns at Angkor Wat.

TIME LINE	40,000BC	10,000	5000	4000	500	AD1	200	4

Ruins of the old Khmer culture at Battambang, Cambodia.

CHRONOLOGY OF EVENTS
AD 802 – 1860

802

The Khmer people were unified by King Jayavarman I to create an empire.

900

The city of Angkor Thom is completed.

1113

Work begins on the building the temple of Angkor Wat.

1150

Angkor Wat is completed.

1181

King Jayavarman VII comes to the throne.

1220

King Jayavarman VII dies.

1500

The Khmer empire comes to an end.

1860

The ruins of Angkor are found again.

an irrigation system ensured three crops a year. The Khmers traded luxury goods with the Chinese, exchanging spices and rhinoceros horn for lacquer ware and porcelain.

Oddly, the Khmer kings were Hindus, while most of the ordinary people were Buddhists. Religious festivals marked the fixed points of the farming year, such as ploughing and harvesting.

Aristocratic women wore skirts but left their upper bodies exposed. Men wore loose loincloths.

Angkor Wat

Angkor Thom was built by 900; Angkor Wat was built between 1113 and 1150. The Khmer empire reached its peaked just after that, during the reign of Jayavarman VII (1181–1220). The huge, impressive and elaborately carved temple complex is surrounded by walls and a moat 4 km long and 180m wide. It consists of three main enclosures symbolizing the outer world, and an inner shrine.

In the fifteenth century invading armies from Thailand forced the Khmers to abandon Angkor. The ruins were swallowed up by the jungle and only found again in 1860.

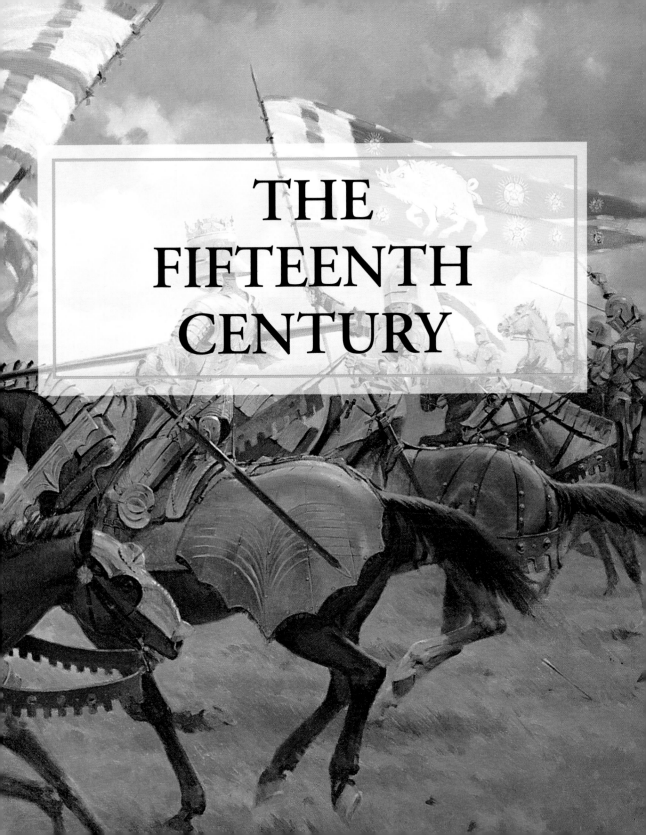

THE
FIFTEENTH
CENTURY

The Fall of Constantinople
AD 1453

OVERVIEW ❖ OVERVIEW ❖ OVERVIEW ❖ OVERVIEW ❖ OVERVIEW

In the fifteenth century in eastern Europe, two great empires came into conflict with each other, the Christian Byzantine empire and the Muslim Ottoman empire. The aggressive new Ottoman empire took over the territories of the Byzantine empire bit by bit until only Constantinople was left – and that was taken in 1453.

Rival empires

In the late middle ages, two great empires were competing for supremacy in eastern Europe. One was the crumbling Byzantine empire, which was Christian, the other was the expanding Ottoman empire, which was Muslim. It was a clash of political power, and also a clash of ideologies. The Ottoman empire had been growing rapidly since 1326, as the Turks conquered more and more of the Byzantine empire. By 1450, much of Greece, Albania, Bosnia and Bulgaria had fallen into their power. The Byzantine empire meanwhile withered away until all that was left was the city of Constantinople.

The attack on Constantinople

Up to 150,000 Turkish troops under Muhammed II made a final and decisive assault on Constanople in 1453. Constantinople was defended by only 10,000 soldiers, under the last Byzantine emperor, Constantine XI, and it is astonishing that they were able to resist the Ottoman force for so long.

The Turks were severely hampered by being unable to take their warships into the Golden Horn, an arm of the sea running through Constantinople; it was guarded well by a huge iron chain. Instead, using manpower with the help of teams of oxen, they dragged 70 galleys (warships propelled by oars) overland to launch an attack. The walls of Constantinople held out for 54

TIME LINE	40,000BC	10,000	5000	4000	500	AD1	200	400

days before Muhammed's elite troops or janissaries broke in and overran the city. The Byzantine empire had been brought to an end, a major landmark in European history.

The Turks converted the great Christian church of St Sophia into a mosque.

The capture of Constantinople – Ottoman Turks invade in 1453.

CHRONOLOGY OF EVENTS
AD 1299 – 1481

1299

The Muslim Ottoman empire is founded by the Turkish Sultan Osman I.

1326

The Ottoman empire starts growing rapidly at the expense of the Byzantine empire.

1413

Muhammed I consolidates the power of the Ottoman empire.

1450

Much of Greece, Albania, Bosnia and Bulgaria has fallen into the power of the Ottomans.

1453

Constantinople was taken by Turkish troops under Muhammed II.

1478

The Turks conquer Albania.

1481

The great Ottoman emperor Sultan Muhammed II, Muhammed the Conqueror, dies aged 51.

Muhammed II, Ottoman sultan who took Constantinople in 1453.

The Hundred Years' War

AD 1337

OVERVIEW ❖ OVERVIEW ❖ OVERVIEW ❖ OVERVIEW ❖ OVERVIEW

In the Hundred Years' War the English kings tried to assert their right to the French throne. Edward III and Henry V tried to conquer France – without success.

Edward III – Coat of Arms.

The English claim

The Hundred Years' War between England and France consisted of several short wars between 1337 and 1453. The kings of England repeatedly attempted to claim the French throne, while the French tried desperately hard to get the English out of France. The dispute dated back to the time of William I, the Duke of Normandy who became King of England.

When Charles IV of France died in 1328 without an heir, the French barons gave the throne to his cousin, Philip IV, but Edward III of England challenged this. Philip's response was to confiscate Edward's French possessions, which led to war. The English fought two famous battles, Sluys and Crecy, but both sides ran out of money and a truce was made in 1347.

In 1355 the English, led by the Black Prince, invaded again, winning the battle of Poitiers and capturing Philip's successor, John II.

Henry V and Agincourt

After a long truce, fighting broke out again in 1415, when Henry V revived the old English claim to the French throne. He captured the port of Harfleur and won the celebrated battle of Agincourt, in which only 1600 Englishmen were killed compared with 10,000 French. The French king, Charles VI was forced to name Henry V as his heir and allow Henry V to marry his (the French king's)

Henry V – Coat of Arms.

TIME LINE	40,000BC	10,000	5000	4000	500	AD1	200	40

daughter, Catherine of Valois. Henry V died a little over a year later, and so was unable to claim the French throne. The Duke of Bedford nevertheless decided to fight on for the French throne on behalf of the infant English king Henry VI.

Joan of Arc

French resistance to this new onslaught was rallied by a 17 year old peasant girl, Joan of Arc (1412–31), who saw visions and heard voices telling her to free France. She succeeded, escorting the uncrowned King of France, Charles VII, to be crowned at Rheims. Shortly afterwards she was captured by Burgundians, sold to the English and burnt as a witch.

Fighting continued for some years, as the English were gradually driven out of France.

Joan of Arc.

CHRONOLOGY OF EVENTS
AD 1328 – 1453

1328

Charles IV of France dies without an heir; the French barons give the throne to his cousin, Philip IV, a decision disputed by the English.

1337

Edward III declares himself King of France. The Hundred Years' War between England and France begins.

1346

Battle of Crecy.

1347

England and France call a truce.

1355

The English, led by the Black Prince, invade France again.

1356

Battle of Poitiers.

1360

Treaty of Bretigny gives England large territories in France.

1415

Fighting breaks out again after a long truce. The Battle of Agincourt.

1431

Joan of Arc is burnt as a witch.

1453

The Hundred Years' War ends. The English are forced out of every part of France except Calais.

Voyages of Discovery (1): Henry the Navigator

AD 1400

OVERVIEW ❖ OVERVIEW ❖ OVERVIEW ❖ OVERVIEW ❖ OVERVIEW

Prince Henry the Navigator founded a school for navigators in Portugal, where voyages along the Atlantic coast of Africa were planned. His initial intention was to reach the treasures of West Africa without crossing the Sahara; later, the aim was to find a sea route to the east and create a new trade route for spices.

Statue of Henry the Navigator, Portuguese prince and patron of explorations.

A school for navigators

Prince Henry the Navigator (1394–1460) was the third son of King John I of Portugal and became governor of the Algarve in 1419. When he was 21 he led an expedition to capture the port of Ceuta in North Africa from the Moors, and in Ceuta he found treasure brought across the Sahara from the River Senegal in West Africa; this made him wonder if the Senegal could be reached by sea.

Between 1424 and 1434, Prince Henry organized 14 voyages along the west coast of Africa. All stopped short of the dangerous waters off Cape Bojador. Sailors were afraid to sail any

| TIME LINE | 40,000BC | 10,000 | 5000 | 4000 | 500 | AD1 | 200 | 40(|

The mistaken belief that the earth was flat led many sailors to fear that they could fall off the edge of the world.

further south. They feared they would fall off the edge of the world, which they thought was flat. They also caught sight of black Africans on the beaches and thought they too would be scorched black by the increasing heat of the sun.

The fifteenth expedition rounded Cape Bojador. Prince Henry was encouraged by this success to found a school of navigation at Sagres on the Portuguese coast where he lived. Here he gathered the best geographers and navigators in Europe to plan future expeditions and train the captains and pilots. A new type of ship was designed, the caravel, a small vessel with lateen (triangular) sails that enabled it to sail into the wind.

Reaching West Africa

By the time Henry the Navigator died in 1460, his ships had reached the coast of Sierra Leone, where the coastline turned eastwards. This gave hope of an easterly run to the Far East. Before the fall of Constantinople in 1453, spices (to improve the taste of salted meat) were taken overland to Constantinople; this made spices very expensive. When Constantinople fell overland trade with the East stopped completely, giving an extra urgency to the voyages of exploration round Africa.

| 600 | 800 | 1000 | 1200 | AD 1400 | 1600 | 1800 | 1900 | 2000 |

Voyages of Discovery (2): Diaz, da Gama & Magellan
AD 1488

OVERVIEW ❖ OVERVIEW ❖ OVERVIEW ❖ OVERVIEW ❖ OVERVIEW

The voyages of discovery were powered by the rediscovery of ancient texts, which made people realise how much there was yet to be discovered. Diaz and da Gama rounded Africa and opened a sea route to the east. Spanish-sponsored explorers, Columbus and Vespucci, sailed west to 'discover' North and South America. The Magellan–del Cano expedition completed the first circumnavigation of the world.

Ptolemy's Celestial Sphere. The Earth is at the centre of the Universe, orbited by the Sun, Moon and planets.

The thirst for new knowledge

The momentum for discovery grew with the rediscovery of classical texts such as Ptolemy's Geography. In the second half of the fifteenth century people were excited by the rediscovery of lost knowledge and fired with a thirst for new knowledge.

Rounding the Cape of Good Hope

It was a disappointment to find the Atlantic coast of Africa turning southwards at the Niger Delta, and it was 1488 before Batholomew Diaz reached and rounded the Cape of Good Hope. Vasco da Gama rounded the Cape in 1497 and reached India, returning home with a cargo of spices. In 1517, Portuguese navigators reached China.

TIME LINE	40,000BC	10,000	5000	4000	500	AD1	200	40

The Spanish–Italian voyages of discovery

While the Portuguese sailed east, the Spanish sailed west. In 1492, Christopher Columbus, a Genoese navigator, was commissioned to cross the Atlantic and reach the Spice Islands (or East Indies). The leading scholars of the day thought the world was round, but smaller than it actually is. Columbus and his sponsors evidently believed he had reached Asia; in fact he had made landfall in the West Indies, part of a 'new' continent previously unknown to Europeans, North America. John Cabot, also Italian, sailed from Bristol in 1497 and discovered Newfoundland.

Another Italian, Amerigo Vespucci, explored the east coast of South America in 1499–1501.

In 1519, Ferdinand Magellan sailed from Spain on the first voyage right round the world. His fleet rounded Cape Horn and crossed the Pacific. Magellan was killed in the Philippines in 1521, but his crew, led by Juan del Cano, arrived back in Spain in 1522.

CHRONOLOGY OF EVENTS
AD 1488 – 1519

1488

Bartholomew Diaz reaches the Cape of Storms, renamed Cape of Good Hope.

1492

Columbus sets sail to cross the Atlantic.

1497

Vasco da Gama rounds the Cape Africa and reaches India.

1497

John Cabot discovers Newfoundland.

1501

Amerigo Vespucci explores the east coast of South America.

1517

Portuguese navigators reach China.

1519

Ferdinand Magellan sails from Spain on the first voyage right round the world, and completes the first circumnavigation in 1522.

Columbus and his fleet in the mid-Atlantic, during their first voyage.

Printing & Books

AD 1440

OVERVIEW ❖ OVERVIEW ❖ OVERVIEW ❖ OVERVIEW ❖ OVERVIEW

The Chinese invented printing in the ninth century, using wood blocks. It was in Europe, where the language required fewer letters, that movable type was invented in the fifteenth century. This made books much cheaper.

A Chinese invention

By AD 1000, the Chinese were printing books using both text and illustrations carved into wood blocks. The earliest known printed book is the Diamond Sutra (868). It took a long time to carve the block for each page, but large numbers of copies could be printed.

Gutenberg and his movable type

In Europe, books were copied by hand for several centuries after this, making books extremely expensive; only the rich could afford them. Block printing was in use in the middle ages to produce single page documents, illustrations and playing cards. In 1440, Johannes Gutenberg invented movable type, separate letters cast in lead alloy which could be used over and over again. This development was made in Europe and not in China, because Chinese consists of thousands of different characters, whereas the European alphabet consists of only 25 letters. Allowing for upper and lower case letters, numbers and punctuation marks, Gutenberg still needed only 300 different pieces of metal type to print his first book, the Bible, in 1456. Pages still needed to be set up letter by letter but, even so, it was quicker than carving wood blocks. Gutenberg also used a printing press adapted from a wine press.

The Chinese were the first to begin printing. The Chinese language is highly complex, using over 2,000 symbols composed of up to 26 strokes each.

TIME LINE	40,000BC	10,000	5000	4000	500	AD1	200	40

A page from Gutenberg's first Bible, of 42 pages.

By 1500 there were nearly 2000 printing presses in Europe, including William Caxton's in London. They had produced 40,000 titles; 20 million books in all were in circulation. This development made possible the rapid spread of information and ideas, one of the foundations of the Renaissance. Aldus Manutius's Aldine Press in Venice produced the first modern printed copies of ancient Greek and Roman texts. Books became cheaper and more accessible. More people learnt to read. The democratization of knowledge was under way.

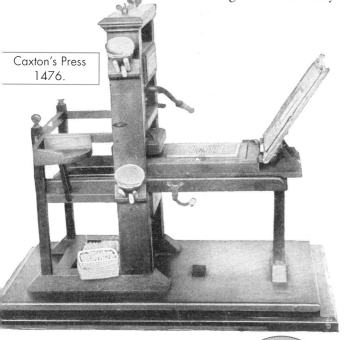

Caxton's Press 1476.

The Renaissance:
Rediscovering Ancient Knowledge
AD 1450

OVERVIEW ❖ OVERVIEW ❖ OVERVIEW ❖ OVERVIEW ❖ OVERVIEW

The rediscovery of pre-Christian scholarship between 1450 and 1600 opened new possibilities, alternatives to the 'truth' taught by the Church in Europe. Humanism and the ideal of the 'Universal Man' were born.

Reviving old scholarship

Throughout the middle ages in Europe, the Church was the main centre for learning, which meant that the Church authorities could exert censorship on learning. In the late fourteenth century, Italian scholars began to rediscover the writings of the ancient Romans and Greeks. When Manuel Chrysoloras became Professor of Greek in Florence in 1397, scholars began to see that pre-Christian writings answered questions that the Church could not. This led to humanism, the belief that people are the mainstay of their own lives and destinies. With this came a determination to establish truths on a scientific basis, and this led to a direct challenge to some of the Church's teachings.

After Constantinople fell in 1453, more scholars arrived in Italy from the east, bringing many old texts with them. The general revival of interest in learning is known as the Renaissance (rebirth).

The development of printing meant that both the ancient texts and ideas about them could spread quickly.

The Universal Man

One ideal in the Renaissance was that of the 'Universal Man' (or Woman), someone who was well-versed in the whole range of arts and sciences. The best-known of these 'Universal Men' is Leonardo da Vinci. He was a brilliant painter and architect, and also a competent engineer, anatomist, botanist, musician and inventor. One idea he was fascinated by was the

TIME LINE	40,000BC	10,000	5000	4000	500	AD1	200	40

possibility that people could fly. He designed a machine called an ornithopter, which consisted of flapping wings; it was an imperfect design, but it anticipated the first successful experiments in flight by nearly 400 years.

Leonardo da Vinci's sketch of a flying machine, circa 1500, which seems in some respects to anticipate our modern-day helicopter, though the technology is not clear.

The Renaissance: Art

AD 1450

Roman architecture was much admired, so Florence cathedral and St Peter's in Rome were fitted with magnificent domes. In the visual arts, realism was the great goal. Wealthy political leaders competed with one another to commission great art from artists such as Leonardo, Michelangelo, Raphael and Botticelli.

Architecture

Another ideal was the revival of classical architecture. The simple, symmetrical lines of classical Greek and Roman buildings were re-created in new buildings such as the Tempietto in Rome, to mark the probable site of St Paul's crucifixion. The dome of Florence cathedral was designed in the 1420s by Filippo Brunelleschi (1377–1446) and completed by 1461. The cathedral tower was so wide that no-one knew how it could be roofed, but Brunelleschi solved the problem after he studied the remains of Roman buildings. Some Roman buildings had survived intact, such as the domed Pantheon in Rome. In 1547, Michelangelo Buonarroti (1475–1564), probably the most brilliant Renaissance artist of all, became the chief architect for St Peter's in Rome, for which he too designed a magnificent dome.

The dome of St. Peter's Basilica in Rome.

Realism and the everyday world

Paintings and sculptures, initially based on classical models, became more realistic. When Michelangelo sculpted Moses, he added veins standing out on the back of his hand. New

TIME LINE	40,000BC	10,000	5000	4000	500	AD1	200	400

refinements in linear and aerial perspective were perfected, to make paintings seem as real as possible. Many art works were still on religious themes, but there were now non-religious or secular subjects too, portraits of merchants and scenes of everyday peasant life.

Wealthy and powerful patrons

Rich and powerful Italian families such as the Borgias and Medicis became major patrons of the arts, commissioning great art and architecture on a grand scale. Lorenzo de Medici (1449–1492) became joint ruler of Florence in 1469; when his brother died he became known as Lorenzo the Magnificent. Under Lorenzo, a clever statesman as well as a great patron of the arts, Florence became the leading city-state in Italy. Popes too commissioned art; Pope Sixtus IV (1414–1484) had the Sistine Chapel designed by Giovanni de Dolci in 1473, and his successor Pope Julius II (1443–1513, pope from 1503) commissioned Michelangelo to decorate the ceiling, work that was done between 1508 and 1512. Commissioning art had become the hallmark of high social status.

This was a period when the visual arts flourished. Great painters such as Breughel, Botticelli, Durer, Holbein, Leonardo, Michelangelo, Raphael and Titian were all at work at this time.

Putti, detail from The Sistine Madonna, 1513, by Raphael.

CHRONOLOGY OF EVENTS
AD 1497 – 1605

1497

Leonardo da Vinci's *The Last Supper*.

1500

Durer's *Self-portrait*.

1504

Michelangelo's *David*.
Leonardo's *Mona Lisa*.

1505

Raphael's *Madonna and Child Enthroned with Saints*.

1508

Michelangelo begins painting the Sistine Chapel ceiling.

1547

Michelangelo becomes the chief architect for St Peter's in Rome.

1565

Brueghel's *Haymaking and Peasant Wedding*.

1600

Shakespeare writes *Hamlet*.

1605

El Greco paints *The Crucifixion*.

The Wars of the Roses
AD 1453

OVERVIEW ❖ OVERVIEW ❖ OVERVIEW ❖ OVERVIEW ❖ OVERVIEW

Two branches of the English royal family, the Plantagenets, fought each other for supremacy between 1453 and 1485, the Houses of York and Lancaster. The Yorkist Protector of the insane Henry VI was challenged by his Lancastrian advisers. The Yorkist Richard III seems to have murdered his own (Yorkist) nephew in order to gain the crown. When Richard III was finally defeated and killed at Bosworth, the victor, Henry Tudor, joined the two families by marrying Edward IV's daughter.

The Plantagenet power struggle

In England a power struggle between two branches of the Plantagenet family, both descended from Edward III, lasted over 130 years. The Wars of the Roses take their name from the emblems of the warring families: the red rose of Lancaster and the white rose of York.

The wars began when Henry VI went mad in 1453 and his cousin Richard Duke of York became Lord Protector. Henry VI's Lancastrian advisers rebelled against Richard of York and his supporters. Richard was killed in the fighting, but in 1461 his son became Edward IV. Henry VI was murdered in the Tower of London at Edward IV's orders in 1471. Edward IV died, suddenly and unexpectedly, in 1483, leaving a young son to succeed him as Edward V. The boy's uncle, Richard Duke of Gloucester, took the boy into custody in the Tower, declaring

TIME LINE	40,000BC	10,000	5000	4000	500	AD 1	200	40

him illegitimate a few weeks later and taking the throne for himself, as Richard III. It is likely that Richard III had his nephew Edward V murdered, along with the king's younger brother, the Duke of York. It has been suggested that he may have been present at Henry VI's death too.

The Battle of Bosworth Field

The remaining Lancastrian heir, Henry Tudor, met Richard III in the Battle of Bosworth Field in Leicestershire in 1485. Richard III was defeated and killed after the Stanley family changed sides during the battle, and Henry Tudor became king as Henry VII.

The Battle of Bosworth Field marked the end of the Wars of the Roses.

CHRONOLOGY OF EVENTS
AD 1453 – 1485

1453
Henry VI has his first bout of insanity, destabilizing the monarchy. A Yorkist Protector, the Duke of York, is challenged by the Lancastrian faction.

1460
Battle of Northampton. Henry VI is taken prisoner.

1461
Battle Towton confirms Edward IV's supremacy.

1470
Henry VI regains his throne briefly.

1471
Battle of Tewkesbury. Prince Edward, Henry VI's son, is stabbed to death by the Dukes of Clarence and Gloucester. Henry VI is executed secretly in the Tower.

1483
Edward IV dies unexpectedly aged 40, succeeded by his twelve year old son Edward V. Edward is declared illegitimate and succeeded by his uncle Richard III.

1485
Battle of Bosworth Field. Richard III is killed. The victor, Henry Tudor, succeeds as Henry VII.

When Henry VII married Elizabeth of York, the daughter of Edward IV, he combined the emblems of the two families to create the Tudor rose, to symbolize the union of the two families.

THE
SIXTEENTH
CENTURY

The Founding of the Mogul Empire

AD 1526

OVERVIEW ❖ OVERVIEW ❖ OVERVIEW ❖ OVERVIEW ❖ OVERVIEW

Babur, an Afghan ruler, invaded northern India in 1526 with assistance from the Ottoman empire and defeated the Indians in battle, becoming the first Mogul (or Mongol) emperor. His grandson Akbar created a great empire stretching from Pakistan to Bangladesh, and was noted for religious tolerance.

Babur, the first Mogul emperor

The Mogul empire was founded in 1526 when Babur, or Babar (1483-1530), a son of the Sultan of Samarkand, defeated the Indian army in the battle of Panipat. Babur had failed to establish himself as ruler of Samarkand, and went to Afghanistan to develop a power base there in 1504. He tried again to take Samarkand in 1511, failed, and then turned his attention towards India when civil war broke out there. He invaded India in 1517.

During the invasion, Babur and his followers were supplied with both arms and troops by the Ottoman empire – because they were Muslims. Babur's invasion also succeeded because his warriors rode horses, which were swift

The Diwan-i-Khas, at Fatehpur Sikri, where Akbar would address the public.

TIME LINE	40,000BC	10,000	5000	4000	500	AD1	200	40

Akbar, wise ruler of the Mogul Empire.

and agile, while the Indians rode slow and ungainly elephants. Babur was able to defeat a much larger Indian army in the battle of Panipat in 1526 and kill the Sultan of Delhi. After this victory Babur became the first Mogul emperor of India and he made Delhi his capital.

The long reign of Akbar

In 1530 Babur died at Agra and was succeeded by his son Humayan, who did not inherit his father's ability and he was chased out of India in 1540. Humayan returned in 1555 to regain his empire, but was killed in the attempt. His 14 year old son Akbar became emperor instead, ruling from 1555 until his death in 1605.

The Mogul empire flourished and grew under Akbar's rule. He was a gifted military leader who was able to conquer Rajputana, Gujarat and Bengal, the richest region in India. Akbar was a wise ruler. Even though he was a Muslim, he recognized that many of his subjects were Hindu and, to ensure peace, he married a Rajput Hindu princess in 1562 and allowed his subjects freedom of worship. He also allowed people to be tried according to their own religious laws. Akbar built a new capital at Fatehpur Sikri, which characteristically combined Hindu and Muslim styles of architecture.

CHRONOLOGY OF EVENTS
AD 1495 – 1605

1495

Babur becomes ruler of Ferghana in Afghanistan.

1504

Babur seizes Kabul in Afghanistan.

1526

Babur invades northern India. Battle of Panipat: Babur is able to defeat a much larger Indian army. Babur founds the Mogul empire.

1530

Babur dies at Agra, succeeded by his son Humayan.

1540

Humayan is chased out of India.

1555

Humayan returns but is killed. His 14 year old son Akbar becomes emperor.

1562

To ensure peace, Akbar marries a Rajput Hindu princess.

1605

Akbar dies.

The Conquistadores & the Fall of Two Empires
AD 1519

Sixteenth century Spanish adventurers based in the Caribbean were able to conquer the Aztec and Inca empires surprisingly easily, partly because they had guns and horses, partly because they were cold-blooded and ruthless.

The fall of the Aztec empire

The arrival of Spanish adventurers called conquistadores (conquerors) led to the downfall of both Aztec and Inca empires. Although their numbers were small, they were ruthless, armed with guns and rode on horses; the native Americans had never seen either before. The conquistadores were motivated entirely by greed. They had heard of the treasure amassed by the Aztec and Inca emperors and were determined to take it.

In 1519 a group of 500 Spanish soldiers under Hernando Cortez (1485–1547) arrived from the Caribbean and attacked the Aztec capital of Tenochtitlan. The Aztec emperor Montezuma II (1466–1520) was waiting for the return of the god-king Quetzalcoatl and assumed that the Spaniards were gods because of their strange clothes. He thought Cortez himself was Quetzalcoatl. Montezuma showered the visiting gods with gifts and willingly stepped aside to allow Cortez to rule in his place. The Aztec people themselves rebelled against Cortez, who retreated to the coast before returning to destroy Tenochtitlan in 1521. After conquering the Aztecs, Cortez returned to Spain, where he died in poverty.

Quetzalcoatl, god-king of the Aztecs, for whom Montezuma mistakenly took Cortez and the Spaniards.

TIME LINE	40,000BC	10,000	5000	4000	500	AD1	200	40

Montezuma, defeated and in chains, kneels before his enthroned conqueror Cortez.

CHRONOLOGY OF EVENTS
AD 1475 – 1547

1475

Francisco Pizarro is born.

1485

Hernan Cortez is born.

1493

Huayna Capac, eleventh emperor of the Incas, is born.

1519

Cortez leads 500 Spanish soldiers from the Caribbean in an invasion of the Aztec empire, attacking the capital, Tenochtitlan. The Aztecs repel Cortez.

1521

Cortez returns to destroy Tenochtitlan and conquer the Aztecs.

1532

Based in the Caribbean, Pizarro invades, and gains control of, Peru.

1541

Pizarro is killed by a rival.

1547

Cortez dies in poverty in Spain.

The fall of the Inca empire

Francisco Pizarro (1475–1541), another conquistador based in the Caribbean, invaded Peru in 1532 with the intention of conquering the Inca empire. The Inca empire in Peru and northern Chile had reached its peak under eleventh ruler, or Sapa Inca, Huayna Capac (1493–1525). On his death in 1525 the empire was divided between his sons Huascar and Atahualpa, which led to a weakening civil war. Atahualpa killed Huascar, then Pizarro captured the Inca capital, Cuzco and imprisoned Atahualpa.

The Inca emperor tried to buy his freedom by filling a room with gold as a ransom, but Pizarro had him executed anyway. Without their king, the Incas quickly surrendered and, within a year of arriving, Pizarro held the Inca empire. He did not enjoy his empire for long. In 1541 he was killed by a rival.

Leonardo & Michelangelo

AD 1452

OVERVIEW ❖ OVERVIEW ❖ OVERVIEW ❖ OVERVIEW ❖ OVERVIEW

The Renaissance is summed up by the wide-ranging talents and sublime art works of two contemporaries, Leonardo and Michelangelo.

Leonardo da Vinci (1452–1519)

Born the illegitimate son of a notary, Leonardo entered the studio of the painter Verocchio in 1470. His first great work, commissioned jointly by Lodovico de Medici and the monks of S Maria delle Grazie, was the mural of *The Last Supper* (1482). This was technically unsatisfactory, a tempera painting on damp plaster, which started deteriorating straight away; it has been restored many times, yet is still regarded as one of the world's masterpieces.

Both Leonardo and Michelangelo were commissioned to decorate the Sala del Consiglio in the Palazzo della Signoria in Florence. Leonardo produced the cartoon (a detailed pencil drawing) of *The Battle of Anghiari*, but once again he used an unsatisfactory paint on plaster technique and gave the project up without finishing it. The *Mona Lisa* was painted in 1504. Among his later works is *The Virgin of the Rocks*.

Just as famous as his paintings are the numerous drawings he made, and which show his wide-ranging abilities as a 'Universal Man'. He had an understanding of science far beyond his time. He wrote notes in mirror writing so that only he could read them.

Leonardo da Vinci, *Self Portrait.*

Michelangelo Buonarotti (1475–1564)

Michelangelo was born in Caprese in Tuscany, where his father was mayor. He was placed in the care of a stonemason at Settignano, where his father owned a marble quarry. In 1488, against his father's advice, Michelangelo became apprenticed to the painter Ghirlandaio, who soon recommended him to Lorenzo de Medici. When Lorenzo died in 1492, his son Pietro showed no interest in Michelangelo, who for a time went to Bologna.

The *Pieta* sculpture (1497) shows a new realism, one of the first expressions of the new humanism. The famous statue of David followed. In 1503, Michelangelo was commissioned to create a tomb for Pope Julius II, but only parts of it were completed, such as the statue of Moses (1513).

Michelangelo is perhaps best remembered for his huge and vivid frescoes in the Sistine Chapel, started in 1508.

Michelangelo's sculpture of *David*.

1452

Leonardo da Vinci is born.

1470

Leonardo enters the studio of the painter Verocchio as an apprentice.

1475

Michelangelo Buonarotti is born in Caprese in Tuscany.

1488

Michelangelo becomes apprenticed to the painter Ghirlandaio.

1497

Leonardo paints his mural of *The Last Supper*.

1504

Leonardo paints the *Mona Lisa*. Michelangelo sculpts *David*.

1508

Michelangelo begins work on the frescoes in the Sistine Chapel.

1513

Michelangelo sculpts Moses.

1519

Leonardo da Vinci dies.

1564

Michelangelo dies.

| 600 | 800 | 1000 | 1200 | AD 1452 | 1600 | 1800 | 1900 | 2000 |

The Reformation

AD 1517

OVERVIEW ❖ OVERVIEW ❖ OVERVIEW ❖ OVERVIEW ❖ OVERVIEW

The Reformation, the campaign to reform the Roman Catholic Church, was begun by Luther in Germany and continued by Zwingli in Switzerland and Knox in Scotland. In England Henry VIII used religious reform as an excuse to sever ties with Rome. The new faith, Protestantism, regarded the Bible, rather than the priest, as the true intermediary with God.

Martin Luther 1483–1546.

Luther, Zwingli, Knox and Henry VIII

The new ideas that were in the air at the time of the Renaissance led some people to challenge the teachings of the Roman Catholic Church. The way of life of the clergy was also denounced. Monks and nuns no longer lived lives of poverty, and bishops and popes lived in luxury. Many thought the Church should be reformed.

The movement known as the Reformation started in 1517, when a priest called Martin Luther nailed a list of 95 statements – all the things he thought were wrong with the Church – to a church door at Wittenberg. Luther was accused of heresy and he was excommunicated (excluded from the Church) in 1521. But Luther by now had supporters in Germany and Switzerland, who set up a new 'Lutheran' Church. From 1529 they were known as 'Protestants'.

In Switzerland, from 1519, the Reformation was led by Ulrich Zwingli, who was more extreme than Luther. He banned the Catholic mass in Zurich, which led to a civil war (1530) between Protestant and Catholic cantons in which Zwingli himself was killed and the Protestants were defeated. John Calvin continued Zwingli's work in Switzerland, while John Knox led the Reformation in Scotland. In England, the Reformation was politically

TIME LINE	40,000BC	10,000	5000	4000	500	AD1	200	40

motivated; Henry VIII was keen to sever ties with Rome when the Pope refused to approve the king's divorce from Catherine of Aragon (1529).

A new faith

The Protestant faith became a major north European phenomenon, spreading from Germany and Switzerland through the Netherlands, England, Wales and Scotland to Scandinavia. A key element in the new religion was the reading of the Bible in the local language, not Latin, so that everyone could understand it, and an emphasis on belief in the Bible rather than on religious ceremonies. The Bible replaced the priest as an intermediary with God.

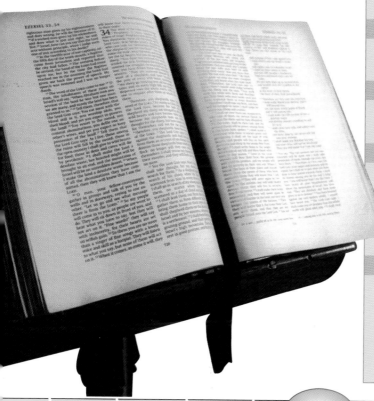

CHRONOLOGY OF EVENTS
AD 1483 – 1529

1483

Martin Luther is born in Eisleben.

1484

Ulrich (or Huldreich) Zwingli is born at Wildhaus.

1507

Luther is ordained.

1513

John Knox, leader of the Scottish Reformation, is born at Haddington.

1517

Martin Luther nails a list of all the things he thinks are wrong with the Church to a church door at Wittenberg.

1519

The Swiss Reformation is led by Ulrich Zwingli.

1520

Luther's supporters in Germany and Switzerland set up a 'Lutheran' Church.

1521

Luther is excommunicated for heresy.

1523

Zwingli's 67 Articles attack the authority of the Pope.

1529

Lutherans become known as 'Protestants'. The Pope refuses to approve Henry VIII's divorce from Catherine of Aragon; Henry VIII is keen to sever ties with Rome.

The Counter-Reformation & the Inquisition

AD 1530

In the 1530s Pope Paul III launched a programme of changes that were intended to reform and strengthen the Catholic Church - the Counter-Reformation. The Inquisition was set up to identify and punish heretics. The movement marked the beginning of a destructive period of religious extremism and persecution.

Capuchins and Jesuits

Pope Adrian VI was the first pope to admit, in 1522, that there was a need for reform in the Roman Catholic Church, but he died before taking any action. In 1534 Paul III became pope and began the reform movement known as the Counter-Reformation. He encouraged the missionary work of the Capuchins, an Italian order of friars, then approved the founding of the Society of Jesus (Jesuits) by Ignatius Loyola (1491–1556). Loyola turned to religion after being wounded in battle. His Society of Jesus was founded with the aim of spreading the Catholic faith, setting up missions in South America, India and China.

A Capuchin Friar, from a a branch of the Order of Franciscans.

The Inquisition

In 1545 Paul III called the Council of Trent, a conference to decide on a

| TIME LINE | 40,000BC | 10,000 | 5000 | 4000 | 500 | AD1 | 200 | 40 |

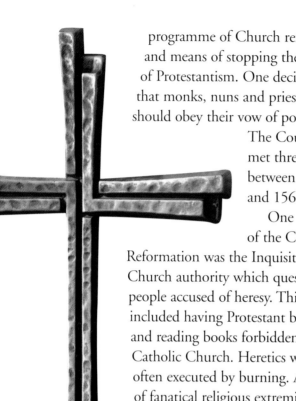

programme of Church reforms and means of stopping the spread of Protestantism. One decision was that monks, nuns and priests should obey their vow of poverty.

The Council met three times between 1545 and 1563.

One product of the Counter-Reformation was the Inquisition, a Church authority which questioned people accused of heresy. This crime included having Protestant beliefs and reading books forbidden by the Catholic Church. Heretics were often executed by burning. A period of fanatical religious extremism followed, in which Catholics persecuted Protestants and Protestants persecuted Catholics. Both joined in persecuting witches; thousands of harmless women were burned or drowned.

In 1554 the heir to the Spanish throne, Phillip, married the Catholic Mary I of England. The marriage failed and when Mary died England became Protestant again under Elizabeth I. Philip, now King of Spain, resolved to make England (and the Netherlands) Catholic by force. His efforts (including the Armada) failed and severely damaged the Spanish economy.

CHRONOLOGY OF EVENTS
AD 1522 – 1588

1522

Pope Adrian VI admits that there is a need for reform in the Roman Catholic Church.

1534

Paul III becomes pope and begins the reform movement known as the Counter-Reformation. The Society of Jesus (Jesuits) is founded by Ignatius Loyola; Loyola has himself been questioned twice by the Inquisition.

1537

The Spanish Inquisition, in existence since the middle ages, is formally developed to ensure Catholic conformity.

1545

Pope Paul III calls the Council of Trent, a conference to decide on a programme of Church reforms and means of stopping the spread of Protestantism.

1554

The heir to the Spanish throne, Philip, marries the Catholic Mary I of England.

1588

Philip, now King of Spain, resolves to make England Catholic by force, sending the Armada.

Copernicus & Galileo

AD 1473

In the Renaissance, some men were starting to question the Christian Church's version of the universe, but fear of the Church stifled debate. Many people, such as Copernicus, did not dare to publish their ideas. By the seventeenth century the Renaissance had spread throughout Europe and initiated a scientific revolution that became known as the Age of Reason, but scientists like Galileo were still punished by the Church for their 'heresies'.

Nicolas Copernicus (1473–1543)

With the birth of humanism came an intense interest in studying the world with a fresh eye. All kinds of new discoveries in geology and astronomy were made, some of them bringing scientists into direct conflict with the Church. Nicolas Copernicus realised that the Earth moved round the Sun, but knew that it was too dangerous to say so. He only published his ideas when he knew he was dying. The Church taught that the earth was the centre of the Universe, and to contradict the Church was to risk imprisonment, torture and death.

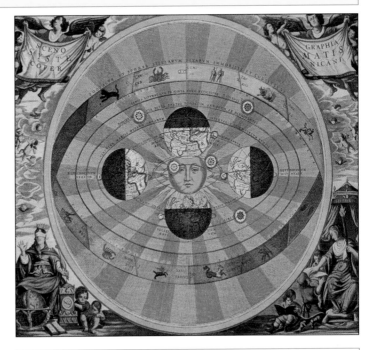

Copernicus's Universe placed the sun at the centre of the universe. There are many similarities between his Universe and the solar system as we see it today.

Galileo supported Copernicus's theory that the earth orbits the sun, and was arrested for his beliefs.

Galileo Galilei (1564–1642)

The Italian astronomer and mathematician Galileo observed the stars using one of the first telescopes in 1610. He made many significant scientific discoveries

He watched the Moon as it changed as it circled the Earth, recognizing that its brightness was not its own; it was lit by the Sun. He also saw that the Moon's surface had valleys and mountains. He drew the surface features he saw through his telescope, (wrongly) interpreting the dark areas as seas, which is why they are still named as seas, such as the Sea of Tranquillity. Galileo discovered that the Milky Way was a track of countless stars, that Jupiter had at least four moons, and that there were spots on the Sun.

In 1632 Galileo bravely published his support of Copernicus. In 1633 he was sentenced to permanent house arrest for his beliefs and forced by the Inquisition to retract his theory that the Earth goes round the Sun. He went on researching until he lost his sight in 1637.

CHRONOLOGY OF EVENTS
AD 1473 – 1642

1473

Nicolas Copernicus is born in Torun, Poland.

1530

Copernicus completes *De Revolutionibus*, proving that the sun is at the centre of the universe, but does not publish it immediately.

1543

Nicolas Copernicus publishes *De Revolutionibus* and dies.

1564

Galileo Galilei is born.

1610

Galileo observes the stars using one of the first telescopes.

1632

Galileo publishes Dialogo, his support of Copernicus.

1633

Galileo is sentenced to house arrest for his beliefs and forced by the Inquisition to retract his theory that the Earth goes round the Sun.

1642

Galileo dies.

Shakespeare & the Theatre

AD 1564

Shakespeare was the outstanding playwright of the Renaissance, producing a large number of plays, some lost, with a wide range of subject and tone - histories, comedies and tragedies. His work is astonishing for the richness of its language and its insight into human nature.

William Shakespeare 1564–1616.

The greatest sixteenth century writer

The Renaissance saw a surge of development in literature. Theatre-going was very popular, and many new plays were written for the many theatres.

The greatest European writer of the sixteenth century was the poet and playwright William Shakespeare (1564–1616), whose work is astonishing for the richness of its poetic language and its full-blooded humanism. He was the son of a rich glover and wool dealer and educated at the local grammar school in Stratford, where he probably saw many plays performed by touring companies. He became an actor in an acting company in London in the 1580s and soon started writing historical plays that were immensely popular and commercially successful, the three parts of *Henry VI* (1592), *Richard III* and *King John*. In 1594, when the theatres re-opened after a two-year closure because of an outbreak of plague, Shakespeare joined the prestigious acting troupe called The Lord Chamberlain's Men, and soon became its joint manager. Between 1593 and 1600 he wrote comedies such as *A Midsummer Night's Dream* and *The Taming of the Shrew*.

TIME LINE	40,000BC	10,000	5000	4000	500	AD1	200	40

When James I came to the throne in 1603, Shakespeare's company became the King's Men. His later plays included tragedies, such as *Hamlet* and *Macbeth*, and he gave much consideration to crafting plays that could be performed with equal success on very different stages. His plays were still performed in open-air theatres like The Globe, but now also indoors in the halls of great houses, where artificial lighting and more elaborate stage effects were possible.

Shakespeare retires

Shakespeare was a very prolific writer, producing 37 plays that have survived and several more that have not. The last play, *The Tempest*, shows a thinly disguised Shakespeare taking his leave of the stage. He formally handed over the role of the King's Men's chief dramatist to John Fletcher and retired in 1612. He died on his birthday, 23 April, St George's Day, in 1616 at his home in Stratford.

The Globe Theatre, South Bank, London.

CHRONOLOGY OF EVENTS
AD 1564 – 1616

1564

William Shakespeare is born at Stratford.

1582

Shakespeare marries Anne Hathaway.

1592

The three parts of *Henry VI*.

1593

Richard III, Comedy of Errors, Venus & Adonis.

1594

Titus Andronicus. The theatres re-open after a two-year closure because of plague.

1597

Romeo and Juliet, Richard II, King John.

1603

Hamlet, All's Well That Ends Well. Shakespeare's company become the King's Men.

1612

Shakespeare retires, formally handing over the role of chief dramatist of the King's Men's to John Fletcher.

1616

Shakespeare dies on his 52nd birthday, St George's Day, at his home in Stratford.

Ivan the Terrible
& Russian Expansion
AD 1533

OVERVIEW ❖ OVERVIEW ❖ OVERVIEW ❖ OVERVIEW ❖ OVERVIEW

In the fifteenth century, Ivan III, Grand Prince of Muscovy, managed to gain independence from the Tartars. During the sixteenth century, his successor, Ivan the Terrible, expanded Russian control eastwards, taking Siberia from the Golden Horde in the 1580s.

Ivan III

Much of southern Russia was controlled by the Mongol rulers of the Tartars (also known as the Golden Horde) in the fifteenth century. In 1462 Ivan III came to the throne of Muscovy, a small princedom centring on the city of Moscow.

Ivan succeeded in gaining independence for his country from the rule of the Golden Horde. In 1472 Ivan married the niece of the last Byzantine emperor and appointed himself protector of the Eastern Orthodox Church, an association that remained with the Russian rulers until the execution of the last Tsar in the twentieth century. Ivan III adopted the double-headed eagle of the Byzantine empire as his emblem.

By 1480 Ivan III had gained control of Novgorod and other cities, calling himself Grand Prince of all Russia and making Moscow his capital. He rebuilt Moscow's citadel, the Kremlin, after it was damaged by fire.

A view of the Kremlin taken from across the river.

TIME LINE	40,000BC	10,000	5000	4000	500	AD1	200	40

Ivan the Terrible

When Ivan died he was succeeded by his son Vasili, who ruled until 1533. He in turn was succeeded by his 3 year old son Ivan IV, who became known as Ivan the Terrible (strictly 'Awe-inspiring') and ruled as Grand Prince of Muscovy for 51 years (1533–1584). Ivan the Terrible was crowned as the first Tsar (emperor) of Russia in 1547.

He reformed the legal system, local government and trading relationships with other European countries. He also expanded his empire by taking Kazan and Astrakhan from the Tartars, even taking Siberia in the 1580s.

He had a brutal and unpredictable personality, killing his eldest son in a fit of rage in 1581. He was succeeded by his second son Fyodor. Boris Godunov acted as regent until Fyodor's death in 1598, then became tsar himself.

CHRONOLOGY OF EVENTS
AD 1462 – 1598

1462

Ivan III is Grand Prince of Muscovy.

1494

Ivan III gains control of Novgorod, calling himself Grand Prince of all Russia.

1505

Ivan dies age 65 and is succeeded by his son Vasili (Basil) III.

1533

Vasili III dies aged 54 and is succeeded by his 3 year old son Ivan IV, later known as Ivan the Terrible.

1547

Ivan IV crowns himself first Tsar of Russia.

1584

Ivan the Terrible dies aged 53, succeeded by his second son, the 27 year old Fyodor.

1598

On Tsar Fyodor's death Boris Godunov becomes tsar.

The Spanish Armada

AD 1588

OVERVIEW ❖ OVERVIEW ❖ OVERVIEW ❖ OVERVIEW ❖ OVERVIEW

The power struggle between Catholic Spain and Protestant England was partly a religious conflict, partly a struggle for supremacy on the high seas. The English provoked Spain by piracy, by alliance with anti-Spanish rebels in the Netherlands and by executing the Catholic Mary Queen of Scots. Philip of Spain launched an invasion fleet against England in 1588, but it was defeated decisively by the English.

The power struggle

In the reign of Elizabeth I of England, some English sailors turned to piracy, attacking Spanish treasure ships bringing silver back to Europe from America. This was a direct challenge to the Spanish assumption of supremacy on the high seas. Then Elizabeth I sent an army to the Netherlands to help the Dutch in their war against Spanish rule. This was a further provocation, which angered Philip II of Spain to the point that he prepared a huge fleet of fighting ships to invade England. Finally, in 1587, Elizabeth I ordered the execution of Mary Queen of Scots. This was portrayed in Spain as the martyrdom of a Catholic queen and gave Philip of Spain the 'just cause' of a holy war. Drake destroyed the Spanish fleet at Cadiz, 'singeing the King of Spain's beard'.

Sir Francis Drake, 1545–1596. English admiral and circumnavigator of the world.

The Spanish Armada

Philip of Spain finally sent his Armada against England in August 1588. He thought his great ships were invincible, but the English captains knew the waters better. Although

TIME LINE	40,000BC	10,000	5000	4000	500	AD1	200	4(

The Spanish Armada. The Spanish Fleet in the Bay of Biscay on its way to attack England.

CHRONOLOGY OF EVENTS
AD 1516 – 1603

1516

Charles V of Spain makes the Netherlands a Spanish possession.

1556

Philip II becomes king of Spain. Fearing Protestantism, Philip tries to extend his power over the Low Countries. Elizabeth I, a Protestant, sends an army to the Netherlands to help the Dutch in their war against Spanish rule.

Feb 1587

Elizabeth I orders the execution of Mary Queen of Scots.

Apr 1587

Drake destroys the Spanish invasion fleet at Cadiz.

Jul 1588

Philip of Spain launches an invasion fleet against England.

Aug 1588

The Spanish Armada is defeated.

1603

Elizabeth I dies, but the war between England and Spain continues intermittently.

the English ships were smaller they were more manoeuvrable than the big Spanish galleons and could 'duck' under the Spanish cannon.

The Armada was decisively defeated in the English Channel by an English fleet commanded by Lord Howard, Sir Francis Drake and Sir John Hawkins. Drake (1543–1596) was already a celebrity after becoming the first Englishman to sail round the world in his ship the Golden Hind in 1580. The English used a system of beacons set up on intervisible hills to send warning of the arrival of the Armada as quickly as possible across country.

The war with Spain continued intermittently until after Elizabeth I's death in 1603.

Folklore states that Drake insisted on finishing a game of bowls at Plymouth Hoe as the Armada was sailing up the British Channel.

The Founding of the Japanese Empire
AD 1568

The one hundred year civil war starting in 1467 in Japan was brought to an end partly by the introduction of firearms from Europe, which enabled small numbers of infantry to defeat much larger cavalry forces armed with bows, arrows and swords. The shogun Hideyoshi (ruled 1585–1598) tried to create a huge Japanese empire, but he failed to conquer China.

The musket. Firearms greatly increased the power of smaller armies against enemies armed only with bows or swords.

Civil war

In 1467 civil war broke out in Japan among the feudal lords. The emperor had lost most of his power and the shogun had little control over events. For over a century private armies of samurai warriors fought each other in the struggle for power. In the midst of this, Europeans arrived bringing Christianity and firearms. Some samurai scorned the new weapons, others quickly saw the advantages. A samurai called Oda Nobunga gave his men muskets and captured Kyoto in 1568. At the battle of Nagashino in 1575, Nobunga armed his 3,000 foot soldiers with muskets, enabling them to defeat a much larger force of mounted samurai armed with bows, arrows and swords.

Hideyoshi and the plan for empire

Nobunga's effort to reunite Japan ended when he was killed, but his work was continued by Toyotomi Hideyoshi, who became shogun (in effect dictator) in 1585. Hideyoshi initially welcomed the Christians because they reduced the power of the Buddhists, whom he

TIME LINE	40,000BC	10,000	5000	4000	500	AD1	200	40

distrusted, but later he realised that Christianity was a threat to Japanese beliefs too. From 1587 Christianity was banned and Christians were put to death. Hideyoshi's ambition was to build a huge Japanese empire that would engulf China. He invaded Korea in 1592 and 1597, but failed to conquer it. The great cost of defeating the Japanese in Korea helped to destabilize China; famine led to unrest and not long after that the Manchus invaded China from the north.

After Hideyoshi's death in 1598, Tokugawa Ieyasu became guardian to Hideyoshi's son, and in effect regent. He withdrew the Japanese forces from Korea after a disastrous campaign costing 260,000 lives. Civil war broke out again, but Ieyasu defeated his enemies at the battle of Sekigahara in 1600. He became shogun in 1603.

Shogun Hideyoshi, who ruled Japan from 1585–1598.

CHRONOLOGY OF EVENTS
AD 1467 – 1603

1467

Civil war among the feudal lords breaks out in Japan.

1568

Oda Nobunga captures Kyoto.

1575

Battle of Nagashino. Nobunga arms his 3,000 foot soldiers with muskets, enabling them to defeat a much larger force of mounted samurai.

1585

Toyotomi Hideyoshi becomes shogun (military dictator) in Japan.

1587

Christianity is banned; Christians are put to death.

1592

Hideyoshi invades Korea.

1597

Hideyoshi invades Korea again, but still fails to conquer it.

1598

Hideyoshi dies, succeeded by his son. Tokugawa Ieyasu becomes regent.

1600

Battle of Sekigahara; Tokugawa Ieyasu defeats his enemies.

1603

Ieyasu becomes shogun.

Renaissance War, Weapons & Armour
AD 1500

OVERVIEW ❖ OVERVIEW ❖ OVERVIEW ❖ OVERVIEW ❖ OVERVIEW

The medieval castle and the siege became obsolete with the increasing use of gunpowder and cannons. Fighting on open battlefields became more common. Ordinary soldiers had poor living conditions and more often died of disease than in battle.

The end of castles

In the middle ages, most fighting took place round heavily fortified castles, and the technique of siege warfare was much the same as it had been in ancient times. Perhaps the greatest siege was the siege of Constantinople in 1453.

By the fourteenth century the use of gunpowder had spread from China to Europe. The invention of cannons and the increasing use of gunpowder meant that castle walls could be knocked down quite easily, and that castles had become obsolete. There were fewer of the long sieges that had been characteristic of the middle ages, more open battles. Cannons and handguns were in use now, adding a third division - artillery - to the traditional two divisions of cavalry and infantry. The early firearms were primitive and unreliable. Matchlocks in the fourteenth century and muskets in the fifteenth century injured the soldiers firing them as often as the enemy; they were also difficult to aim accurately.

Arundel Castle in West Sussex.

TIME LINE	40,000BC	10,000	5000	4000	500	AD1	200	40

Armies, arms and armour

Most armies in Europe consisted of full-time professional soldiers. They were often hired out by their kings as mercenaries, many of which worked well outside Europe and as far afield as South-East Asia. Soldiers were usually underpaid and underfed, living in poor and unsanitary conditions, more often dying of disease than in battle. Kings also functioned as commanders-in-chief of their armies and still, as in the middle ages, attended on the battlefield. The King of Portugal was killed in battle against the Moroccans in 1578.

Firearms were only introduced into Japan towards the end of the sixteenth century, so castles such as Hideyoshi's were still important there.

European knights and their horses wore heavy and elaborately crafted plate armour. Fully armoured knights were so heavy that they had to be lifted onto their horses with a winch. This was dangerous, as once they were knocked off their horses they were unable to remount, or even get up off the ground.

CHRONOLOGY OF EVENTS
AD 1350 – 1550

1350
Gunpowder comes into use in Europe. From now on sieges become shorter and there are more open battles. Castles also become less useful.

1400
Suits of armour remain simple: a conical 'pig-faced' basinet helmet, with chain mail to protect the body.

1430
The hulls of Spanish ships are sheathed in metal armour.

1453
Siege of Constantinople, the last of the long sieges.

1460
Full suits of plate armour appear.

1540
The finest suits of armour are made. The armourer's craft reaches its peak.

1550
The King of Portugal is killed in battle against the Moroccans.

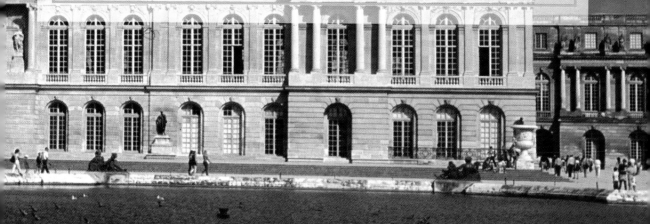

THE
SEVENTEENTH
CENTURY

The Pilgrim Fathers & the English Colonies in North America

AD 1600

The first English colonies in North America ran into difficulties, with food shortages, disease and conflict with native Americans accounting for many deaths. The first successful colony at Jamestown, Virginia (1607), was followed by others, including Plymouth, New England (1620), founded by the Pilgrim Fathers.

An English Puritan.

English colonies

For most of the sixteenth century, Europeans regarded North America as an obstacle that was in the way of trade with the Far East. It was not until a hundred years after Columbus that they realised the land might be a valuable resource in itself. The first successful English colony was set up at Jamestown in Virginia in 1607. Food shortages, disease and conflict with the native Americans nearly wiped it out, but it was saved by its leader, Captain John Smith. The colonists started growing tobacco as a cash crop, and they began to prosper. The demand for tobacco grew and the colonists took more land from the native Americans. This inevitably led to a struggle for land.

The Mayflower

The Mayflower sailed from Plymouth in England in 1620, taking 102 Puritans to North America. Religious intolerance in England forced

TIME LINE	40,000BC	10,000	5000	4000	500	AD1	200	4

The Mayflower II, replica of the Pilgrim Fathers' ship.

CHRONOLOGY OF EVENTS
AD 1584 – 1620

1584

The first English colony, on Roanoke Island, is named Virginia by Walter Raleigh.

May 1607

The first successful English colony in North America is founded at Jamestown, Virginia, by Captain Christopher Newport.

Dec 1607

Captain John Smith, left in charge by Newport, trades with the Algonquin Indians for food; the colonists are starving.

Sep 1608

Newport returns to Jamestown with fresh supplies.

1610

The Jamestown give up their colony but are persuaded to return when they meet the Virginia, carrying 150 new colonists.

16 Sep 1620

The Mayflower sails from Plymouth in England taking 102 Puritans.

11 Nov 1620

Plymouth, New England founded by the Pilgrim Fathers.

them to seek a new land where they could worship as they wished. In 1620, the Pilgrim Fathers landed near Cape Cod, founding a small colony that they named Plymouth. This settlement was the first successful colony in New England and its founding is regarded as the beginning of the Unites States. By 1700 there were so many Europeans in North America that they had begun to take the continent over from the Native North Americans.

Thanksgiving

But the colonists were ill prepared for life in a wilderness, or for the bitter cold of the New England winters. Food supplies ran out. Many of the colonists died of hypothermia and disease during the first winter. Only 54 of them were still alive in the spring of 1621. The first Thanksgiving Day, in 1621, was a heartfelt celebration of the Pilgrim Fathers' first successful harvest. Thanksgiving Day is still celebrated every year – throughout America.

Cardinal Richelieu & the Greatness of France
AD 1624

OVERVIEW ❖ OVERVIEW ❖ OVERVIEW ❖ OVERVIEW ❖ OVERVIEW

Cardinal Richelieu was Louis XIII's first minister from 1624 until his death in 1642. He worked to destroy all who opposed him in France, including the Huguenots (Protestants), and pursued a vigorous warlike foreign policy that made France a great power. Richelieu was, even so, much feared and hated in France.

Cardinal Richelieu

When Henry IV of France was assassinated in 1610, he was succeeded by his 9 year old son, Louis XIII, with his mother, Marie de' Medici, as regent. In 1614, Armand Duplessis (later Cardinal Richelieu,1585–1642) became adviser to the queen, then in 1616 he was promoted to secretary at war and for foreign affairs. Richelieu was a priest as well as a politician, and he returned to his diocese (Lucon) for a time. In 1622 he was created a cardinal. He also saw himself as a dramatist.

When Louis XIII reached his majority he appointed Richelieu as his minister of state (1624). Richelieu may have been grandee of the Church, but his true ambition was the aggrandisement of France. He destroyed his rivals within France, ruled harshly and pursued an aggressive foreign policy.

The Huguenots

In 1628, Richelieu personally oversaw the suppression of the Huguenots, the French Protestants who had for long resisted the king's power. He destroyed their stronghold at La Rochelle after a year-long siege which starved them out. Richelieu later destroyed the final Huguenot refuge at Montauban. The Protestants were now too weak to cause Richelieu further trouble.

| **TIME LINE** | **40,000BC** | **10,000** | **5000** | **4000** | **500** | **AD1** | **200** | 4 |

He appointed intendants who toured the country, supervising taxation, policing and the law courts. They acted as spies, reporting any subversive activity. Anyone plotting against Richelieu risked prison and possibly death.

In 1631, when Habsburg Austria had overrun Germany and threatened the whole of Europe, Richelieu paid Denmark, Sweden and the Netherlands to fight the Habsburgs. In 1635 Richelieu opened a war with Spain, which continued after his death, but by then the French army had proved itself one of the best in Europe. Richelieu succeeded in establishing France as a great European power, but he was deeply hated by the French people – and for his harshness, not for his bad plays.

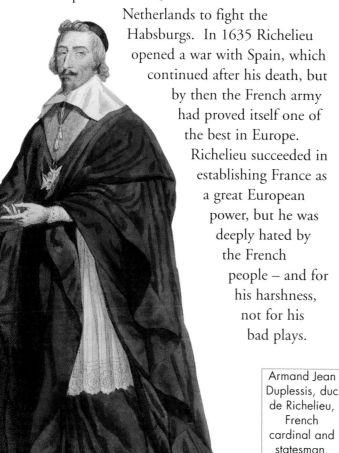

Armand Jean Duplessis, duc de Richelieu, French cardinal and statesman.

CHRONOLOGY OF EVENTS
AD 1585 – 1642

1585

Richelieu is born as Armand Jean Duplessis.

1610

Henry IV of France is assassinated, succeeded by his nine year old son, Louis XIII, with his mother, Marie de' Medici, as regent.

1614

Cardinal Richelieu becomes adviser to the Queen.

1622

Richelieu is created a cardinal.

1624

Richelieu becomes Louis XIII's first minister.

1628

Richelieu personally oversees the suppression of the Huguenots in a year long siege at La Rochelle which starves them out.

1631

Richelieu pays Denmark, Sweden and the Netherlands to fight the Habsburgs.

1634

Richelieu founds the French Academy.

1635

Richelieu opens a war with Spain.

1642

Richelieu dies.

Improving Communications

AD 1600

European travel improved in the seventeenth century, with cabs to transport people within cities, horse-drawn coach services connecting the major cities with one another, and ships and barges transporting goods by sea, river and canal. Postal services were introduced – and the first newspapers.

Travel

Travel overland in Europe became faster, more comfortable and more reliable in the seventeenth century. Within cities sedan chairs were available for wealthy people to hire to take them through the muddy streets. The first hackney coaches appeared in London in 1620. The first four-wheel cabs (fiacres) appeared in Paris in 1650.

Horse-drawn coach services connected the major towns, and it was possible to travel up to 40 miles a day. Ships took raw materials and heavy goods round the coasts, and barges took them inland along rivers and linking canals.

A French carrosse –
the earliest type of private carriage.

TIME LINE	40,000BC	10,000	5000	4000	500	AD1	200	40

Postal services

Letters were carried short distances, within cities, by couriers on foot, and longer distances on horseback, using relays of post-horses. Regular correspondence between scholars and merchants was now possible, bringing huge benefits to scholarship and trade. A network of postal agreements was set up in western Europe in 1601, a parcel post was started in France in 1643, and a Penny Post was started in England in 1680.

Newspapers

Many people could not read and relied on being told the news. The authorities in Europe's towns and cities were responsible for informing people about important

events. A drummer brought people out into the street, where a town crier read the news aloud to them. Business news was often passed on in coffee houses in both Europe and North America, where politicians as well as businessmen met to relax and discuss the affairs of the day.

In the seventeenth century the first newspapers appeared. The earliest was *New Tidings*, published in Antwerp. Another early paper, the *Antwerp Gazette*, consisted of a single sheet, with a picture and an outline of the main news story. The first issue of the *Paris Gazette* came out in 1631. London's first newspaper, the *Daily Courant*, was founded in 1702.

CHRONOLOGY OF EVENTS
AD 1601 – 1702
1601
A network of postal agreements is set up in western Europe.
1604
Work on the Briare Canal linking the Rivers Loire and Seine is started.
1605
The first railway is installed in a coal mine at Woolaston, Nottinghamshire.
1605
The earliest newspaper *New Tidings*, is published in Antwerp.
1609
Regular newspapers appear in Saxony and Strasbourg.
1617
The first one-way street system is created in London.
1620
The first hackney coaches appear in London.
1680
A Penny Post is started in England.
1702
London's first newspaper, the *Daily Courant*, is founded.

The Dutch Empire

AD 1600

OVERVIEW ❖ OVERVIEW ❖ OVERVIEW ❖ OVERVIEW ❖ OVERVIEW

The Dutch founded two great trading companies. The Dutch East India Company controlled the spice trade from the east. The Dutch West India Company controlled the sugar, tobacco and slave trade from the Caribbean and founded New Amsterdam on the Hudson River, which in 1664 was taken by the English and renamed New York. The Dutch became very rich on the proceeds of this commercial empire.

The Dutch East India Company

The English East India Company was formed in 1600, but there was strong competition for trade in the Far East and the Dutch East India Company was set up two years later. These organizations became very powerful, arming their ships and maintaining private armies to defend them; they had military bases as well as trading bases; they fought against surrounding countries and made treaties with them. They behaved in effect like sovereign states.

The Dutch won the power struggle to control the spice trade, and the defeated English turned their attention to India, where the Mogul rulers were content to give them trading rights.

The Dutch East India Company's military strength was such that it was able to drive out the Portuguese and the

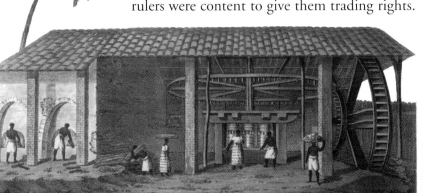

Slaves working in a Sugar Mill in the West Indies.

TIME LINE	40,000BC	10,000	5000	4000	500	AD1	200	40

The spice trade was controlled by the Dutch East India Company.

CHRONOLOGY OF EVENTS
AD 1600 – 1664

1600

The English East India Company is founded.

1602

The Dutch East India Company is founded.

1616

The Dutch Captain Hartog makes the first European landing on the west coast of Australia.

1621

The Dutch West India Company is founded.

1622

The Dutch make several landfalls on the south-east coast of Australia.

1624

The Dutch found the New Netherland colony on the Hudson River with a trading post called New Amsterdam on Manhattan Island.

1647

Peter Stuyvesant becomes the governor of New Amsterdam.

1652

The Dutch East India Company occupies the Cape of Good Hope.

1664

New Amsterdam on the Hudson River is taken by the English and renamed New York.

English, seize Ceylon (Sri Lanka) and, in 1652, occupy the Cape of Good Hope as a staging post between Europe and the East.

The Dutch West India Company

In 1621 the Dutch West India Company was founded. Shortly after that as many as 800 Dutch vessels were trading sugar, tobacco, hides and slaves from the Caribbean. The Dutch founded a colony in Guiana and occupied north-east Brazil. In 1624 they founded the New Netherland colony on the Hudson River, with a trading post called New Amsterdam on Manhattan Island. Its harsh governor from 1647 to 1664 was Peter Stuyvesant, who was hated equally by the native Americans and the colonists; in 1664, the colonists were happy to surrender to a small English fleet, who renamed the colony New York.

The seventeenth century was a golden age for the Dutch. As their commercial empire expanded, they came to enjoy the highest standard of living in the world.

The tobacco trade was controlled by the Dutch West India Company.

The English Civil War

AD 1642

OVERVIEW ❖ OVERVIEW ❖ OVERVIEW ❖ OVERVIEW ❖ OVERVIEW

The Civil War (1642–1651) was a major ideological struggle between those who believed in the absolute authority of the monarchy and those who believed in the authority of Parliament. Initially there was no intention of getting rid of either the king or the monarchy, but Charles I would not accept defeat; in the end executing him seemed the only solution. There was no obvious alternative form of government to monarchy, and Oliver Cromwell became Lord Protector, a kind of constitutional monarch. The (possibly premature) experiment did not last long and Charles I's son was recalled from exile.

The Civil War

Charles I (1600–1649) believed in the divine right of kings; he was not responsible to Parliament. This led to a civil war between the king's supporters, Royalists, and the supporters of Parliament, Parliamentarians. Charles I tried to rule without Parliament from 1629 to 1640, only recalling it to ask for money to suppress a rebellion in Scotland. The physical fighting began in 1642, with the Battle of Edgehill, and at first the King had the advantage. As the war continued the superior training (and funding) of the Parliamentarian army had its effect. Oliver Cromwell's New Model Army decisively defeated Charles I's army at the Battle of Naseby in 1645.

Charles was held under house arrest at a number of locations, but he refused to accept defeat. While he was in prison at Carisbrooke Castle on the Isle of Wight, he tried to negotiate with the Scots,

Oliver Cromwell 1599–1658.

TIME LINE	40,000BC	10,000	5000	4000	500	AD1	200	40

who he hoped would reopen the war on his behalf. This led to a brief second civil war breaking out, but it was quickly brought to an end. Parliament had no choice but to bring the King to trial for treason. He was condemned to death and beheaded in 1649. The Royalists fought on for a time. After the Battle of Worcester (1651), the last battle, the dead king's heir, Charles II, had to leave the country.

The Protectorate and the Restoration

The execution of the King led to confusion. Several solutions were tried. In 1653, Oliver Cromwell (1599–1658) became Lord Protector. He was King in all but name, and he was offered the crown. In 1658, Cromwell died and his less able son Richard Cromwell succeeded him. He was removed by the army, who invited Charles II to return from exile. This resumption of the monarchy in 1660 is known as the Restoration.

Charles I 1600–1649.

1625

Charles I becomes king, aged 27.

1629

Charles I begins to rule without Parliament.

Nov 1640

The King recalls Parliament (Long Parliament) to ask for money to suppress a rebellion in Scotland.

July 1641

The Long Parliament abolishes the Star Chamber in an effort to curb Charles I's absolutism.

23 Oct 1642

The Civil War begins. The Battle of Edgehill is won by the Royalists.

14 Jun 1645

Battle of Naseby. Oliver Cromwell's New Model Army defeats Charles I's army.

30 Jan 1649

Charged with treason, Charles I is executed outside the Banqueting House, Whitehall.

1653

Oliver Cromwell becomes Lord Protector.

3 Sep 1658

Cromwell dies, succeeded by his son Richard Cromwell.

7 May 1659

The Rump Parliament meets to force Cromwell's resignation.

8 May 1660

The Restoration: Charles II is proclaimed King.

| 600 | 800 | 1000 | 1200 | 1400 | AD 1642 | 1800 | 1900 | 2000 |

Baroque Architecture: the Spirit of Fearlessness
AD 1600

OVERVIEW ❖ OVERVIEW ❖ OVERVIEW ❖ OVERVIEW ❖ OVERVIEW

The Baroque style borrowed symmetry and classical architectural detail from the Renaissance, but added a new recklessness in scale. Many spectacular public buildings – cathedrals, palaces and public squares - were designed by great architects such as Bernini and Wren.

Versailles and St Peter's Square

The seventeenth century style of European architecture is known as Baroque. Grandiose public buildings were designed by great architects such as Giovanni Lorenzo Bernini and Francesco Borromini in Italy, Inigo Jones, Christopher Wren, Nicholas Hawksmoor and John Vanbrugh in England.

Louis XIV's palace at Versailles, France.

The most spectacular single building was Louis XIV's palace at Versailles, where work began in 1662 under the architect Jules Hardouin-Mansart (1645–1708). The Orangery (1685) is the finest part. The spectacular formal gardens at Versailles were designed by Andre Lenotre (1613–1700), who was also commissioned to design St James's Park and Kensington Gardens in London. These buildings were rigorously and emphatically symmetrical and most

| TIME LINE | 40,000BC | 10,000 | 5000 | 4000 | 500 | AD1 | 200 | 4(|

of the detail, such as triangular pediments over the windows, was classical in origin, showing a Renaissance origin. But there was also a certain recklessness about the new style. Even the smaller buildings, such as the Bodleian Library in Oxford (1615) succeeded in being challenging and imposing. The Banqueting House in Whitehall was designed by Inigo Jones (1573–1652)and completed in 1622. In 1629, Bernini (1598–1680) became architect at St Peter's in Rome, designing the baldacchino and facade for the basilica, the colonnade for St Peter's Square and many other buildings in Rome.

Rebuilding Paris and London

When Old St Paul's Cathedral was destroyed in the Great Fire of London in 1666, Christopher Wren (1632–1723) was commissioned to design a replacement. His initial design, with a plan in the shape of a Greek cross (arms of equal length), was rejected as too daring and Wren was forced to add a conventional nave. Building began in 1675.

Cities such as Paris and London were substantially rebuilt in the new style, fire-proof brick and stone replacing timber. Often the facing stonework was finely decorated with carvings. Scarcity of land in Amsterdam dictated that building plots had to be narrow. There was no space to waste between houses, so even the higher-status dwellings were joined side by side to make terraces. Perhaps the greatest private building in the Baroque style is Blenheim Palace, designed for the Duke of Marlborough by John Vanbrugh in 1705.

St Paul's Cathedral, London.

CHRONOLOGY OF EVENTS
AD 1615 – 1705

1615

The Bodleian Library in Oxford is built.

1622

The Banqueting House in Whitehall is designed by Inigo Jones.

1633

Baldacchino, St Peter's Basilica, Rome, designed by Bernini.

1638

Covent Garden: the first planned piazza in London is designed by Inigo Jones.

1675

St Paul's Cathedral in London; building begins under Christopher Wren.

1662

Louis XIV's palace at Versailles work began under Hardouin-Mansart.

1687

Kensington Palace, London, designed by Christopher Wren.

1705

John Vanbrugh designs Blenheim Palace.

Witch Trials & Superstitions

AD 1600

OVERVIEW ❖ OVERVIEW ❖ OVERVIEW ❖ OVERVIEW ❖ OVERVIEW

Many superstitions survived into the Age of Reason. In some rural areas in Europe whole villages followed the pre-Christian religion of their remote ancestors. When conflict broke out between Catholics and Protestants in the sixteenth and seventeenth centuries, these alleged 'Devil-worshippers' were persecuted, tortured and executed.

Old beliefs and witch trials

The Age of Reason, with its scientific discoveries, did not do away with old superstitions dating back to the middle ages and earlier. Thousands of people still took children with skin complaints to be touched by the monarch. 'The King's touch' was believed to have a magic healing effect.

People still believed that everyday events were specific acts of God, rewards or punishments for good or evil actions. When things went wrong for the whole community, such as a crop failure, someone within the community must be held to account.

The religious conflicts of the sixteenth century, between Catholics and Protestants, created a hysteria that led to both sides persecuting people they regarded as witches. In the later seventeenth century too, thousands of people in England and New England were tried and executed for witchcraft. In most countries religious laws were passed, requiring people to worship in a particular way; in Christian countries in Europe, church attendance was compulsory. The Puritan migrants to North America became as intolerant as the authorities they had left in Europe.

In 1692 several girls at Salem in Massachusetts said they had been bewitched by a West Indian slave. This led to a witch craze, a witchcraft trial and the hanging of 19 women.

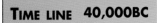

TIME LINE	40,000BC	10,000	5000	4000	500	AD1	200	40

The Old Religion

There were genuine witches, 'wise people' who were practising a pagan religion dating back to pre-Christian days. In some areas, especially remote rural areas, whole villages followed the practices of their ancestors. The pagan deity was often portrayed as an animal-god, represented by a man in an animal mask; this dates back more than 7,000 years. The stag headdress with its horns led the Christian recorders of the religion in the middle ages to identify this god as the Devil. Inevitably, when the Christian Church was divided and both Catholics and Protestants felt threatened, those thought to be followers of the Old Religion were ferociously persecuted.

Three witches are burned in the Harz Mountains, Germany.

CHRONOLOGY OF EVENTS
AD 1200 – 1712

Circa 1200

First witch trials in England.

1315

In France, several people are charged with using enchantments against Louis X. One witch is burnt; de Marigny, one of the King's ministers, is hanged.

1324

Witches in Coventry are accused of trying to kill Edward II by plunging daggers into wax images. The trial is abandoned.

1372

Pope Gregory XI authorizes the Inquisition to deal with sorcerers and magicians.

1483

Lord Hastings, who espouses the cause of the Princes in the Tower, is beheaded for witchcraft at Richard III's orders.

1484

Pope Innocent VIII issues a bull against witchcraft.
Kramer and Sprenger publish their witch-hunters' manual, *Malleus Maleficarum*.

1692

The Salem witch craze. 19 women are hanged for witchcraft.

1712

The last prosecution in England under the witchcraft acts.

The Slave Trade

AD 1600

OVERVIEW ❖ OVERVIEW ❖ OVERVIEW ❖ OVERVIEW ❖ OVERVIEW

The slave trade was well established in Africa centuries before the Europeans arrived and started transporting ship-loads of African slaves to the New World. In the sixteenth century the English began trading in a 'Slave Triangle'; cloth and goods from England to Africa, slaves to the Caribbean, sugar, tobacco and later cotton to England. The Europeans saw nothing wrong in treating people in this barbaric and cruel way.

African and Portuguese slavers

The first African slaves were taken to America as early as 1502, but the slave trade was already part of the African culture. In the tenth century, when the kingdom of Ghana was at its peak, people captured in southern Africa were taken to Ghana and sold as slaves. Arab traders bought them, took them across the Sahara and sold them on to wealthy people in the Mediterranean and Middle East. European slavers often dealt with West African chiefs who were happy to sell their own captives. People were already regarded as a commodity.

Portuguese colonists in the Moluccas used local slave labour to harvest nutmeg and cloves. The Portuguese initially set up colonies on the Atlantic coast of Africa. They had sugar plantations on the island of Sao Tome, but after a slave revolt there in the 1570s they set up new sugar plantations in Brazil, transporting slaves across the Atlantic to work there. Slaves were often fitted with spiked iron collars to stop them escaping. The Portuguese empire was based on slavery. Colonists in Brazil and India lived in great luxury, surrounded by low-paid servants.

Slaves were taken from Ghana, across the Sahara, to the Mediterranean and Middle East.

TIME LINE	40,000BC	10,000	5000	4000	500	AD1	200	40

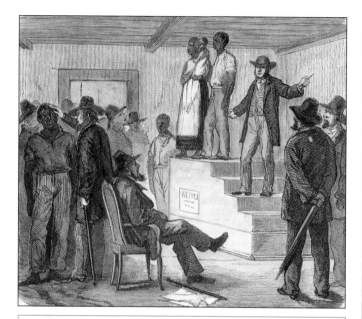

A slave sale in America.

CHRONOLOGY OF EVENTS
55 BC – AD 1786

55 BC

Julius Caesar sells 63,000 Gauls into slavery, part of a regular commerce in slaves in the Roman world.

AD 950

The kingdom of Ghana is at its peak. People captured in southern Africa are taken to Ghana and sold as slaves. The slave trade is already part of the African culture.

1494

Columbus sends back to Spain 500 Indian prisoners to be sold as slaves in Seville.

1502

The first African slaves are taken to the Americas.

1562

John Hawkins buys slaves in Sierra Leone and takes them to Hispaniola. This is the beginning of the English Slave Triangle.

1786

The peak of the slave trade. 2,130,000 slaves have been transported to British colonies in America in the last hundred years.

The English and their Slave Triangle

The English became involved in the slave trade under Elizabeth I. In 1562 John Hawkins bought slaves in Sierra Leone, took them to Hispaniola, where he traded them for sugar and hides, which he took back to England. This was the beginning of the Slave Triangle; typically a voyage might start from Bristol, taking cloth and manufactured goods to West Africa, slaves to Jamaica or Florida, sugar, tobacco and later cotton to England.

The living conditions for the slaves were terrible. A third of them died on the voyage across the Atlantic. Another third died within three years of landing because of disease, the brutality of their owners or general neglect. The Europeans regarded Africans as sub-human and saw nothing wrong with treating them in this way.

Louis XIV & Absolutism

AD 1638

OVERVIEW ❖ OVERVIEW ❖ OVERVIEW ❖ OVERVIEW ❖ OVERVIEW

Louis XIV (1638–1715) was a master of self-publicity, cultivating an image of regal splendour which has never been surpassed. With his magnificent palace of Versailles and his absolute power, he became known as le Roi Soleil, the Sun King. His was the longest reign in European history (1643-1715).

Absolute monarchy

When Louis XIII died in 1643 he was succeeded by his son Louis XIV, who was only 5. Louis XIV's mother, Anne of Austria, ruled on his behalf together with her lover, Cardinal Mazarin, until 1651, Mazarin continuing in power until 1661. The burden of heavy taxes caused the people of Paris to rise in a revolt called the Fronde in 1648 and Louis XIV was forced to leave the city for a time. The Fronde collapsed in 1652 and Louis XIV returned to an enthusiastic welcome. He decided that he would make sure nothing like the Fronde would ever happen to him again. It was in 1661, when Mazarin died, that Louis took over the government of France and turned it into an absolute monarchy, with the power totally concentrated in his own hands. Louis XIV once said, 'L'état c'est moi': 'The state? I am the state.'

Louis XIV appointed Jean Colbert as Controller-General of Finance. Colbert turned France into the most efficiently run state in Europe. He set up industries, had new roads, bridges and canals built, and expanded the navy. In 1662 Louis XIV bought the 200 year old Gobelins factory in Paris, turning it into a fine arts factory producing tapestries that glorified the King.

The lavish hospitality offered at the palace of Versailles was also intended to promote this image of regal magnificence, impressing French

TIME LINE	40,000BC	10,000	5000	4000	500	AD1	200	40

Louis XIV,
King of France,
in theatre costume
as Le Roi Soleil
– the Sun King.

subjects and foreign ambassadors alike.

The new palace was built just outside Paris, for security reasons; after the Fronde Louis did not trust the Parisians enough to want to live in the capital. The palace, which took 36,000 men 47 years to complete, was surrounded by magnificent formal gardens.

Louis XIV was like the Sun, with the whole of France revolving round him. That, and his dazzling splendour in his youth and middle years, earned him the title 'the Sun King'. In old age he degenerated into a gloomy tyrant; for his subjects, he lived too long.

CHRONOLOGY OF EVENTS
AD 1638 – 1715

1638

Louis XIV is born at St Germain-en-Laye.

1643

Louis XIII dies, succeeded by his 5 year old son Louis XIV.

1648

The Fronde revolt begins.

1651

Louis XIV's mother, Anne of Austria, dies. She has ruled on Louis's behalf together with her lover, Cardinal Mazarin.

1652

The Fronde collapses.

1661

Mazarin dies. Louis takes over the government of France.

1711

Louis's eldest son, the Dauphin, dies.

1712

Louis's eldest grandson, the Duke of Burgundy, dies.

1715

Louis XIV dies. His reign is the longest recorded in European history.

The Authorized Version
of the Bible
AD 1611

Translating the Bible into English was for a long time illegal. By 1604, the need for an agreed and reliable translation was seen. The Authorized Version appeared in 1611.

The Authorized Version

James I of England (and VI of Scotland) sanctioned an official English translation of the Bible. This has become known as the Authorized Version (or sometimes the King James Version) and is generally regarded, along with the plays of Shakespeare's maturity, as one of the greatest achievements of Jacobean England.

A conference of leading English Christians at Hampton Court in 1604 concluded that a new and reliable translation of the Bible was essential. The King approved and work began. Fifty scholars worked on the project for the biblical seven years, and the new translation was published in 1611.

William Tyndale and Miles Coverdale

The Bible had been translated before, but illegally. In the sixteenth century both Tyndale and Coverdale risked their lives to translate the Bible. Making the Bible directly accessible to ordinary people was seen by the Church authorities as an act of subversion.

TIME LINE	40,000BC	10,000	5000	4000	500	AD1	200	4

William Tyndale (1494–1536) was unable to find support in England for his translation of the New Testament in 1524. He left in fear of his life, visiting Luther in Wittenberg before getting his Bible published in Worms in 1526. In England his work was denounced by powerful enemies including Sir Thomas More. It was probably More who plotted his capture in Antwerp, where he was tried and burned alive in 1536.

Ironically, only the year before, Miles Coverdale (1488–1568) had published the first translation of the whole Bible into English in Zurich. Times were changing. In 1539 the Great Bible, edited by Coverdale, was published in London under the patronage of Thomas Cromwell. Coverdale survived, but had to leave England when the Catholic Mary I came to the throne. Much of Tyndale's and Coverdale's work found its way into the Authorized Version.

'In the beginning was that word, and that word was with god: and god was that word. The same was in the beginning with god. All things were made by it, and without it was made no thing that was made. In it was life. And life was the light of men, and the light shineth in darkness, and darkness comprehended it not.'

These are the words of Tyndale, martyred for making the Bible accessible to ordinary people.

1488

Miles Coverdale is born.

1494

William Tyndale is born.

1524

William Tyndale completes his translation of the New Testament.

1526

Tyndale's Bible is published in Worms.

1535

Coverdale's Bible, the first translation of the whole Bible into English, is published in Zurich.

1536

William Tyndale is captured in Antwerp and burnt alive.

1539

The Great Bible, edited by Coverdale, is published in London.

1568

Miles Coverdale dies.

1604

The Hampton Court conference concludes that there is a need for an agreed translation. James I sanctions an official English translation.

1611

The Authorized Version appears.

| 00 | 800 | 1000 | 1200 | 1400 | AD 1611 | 1800 | 1900 | 2000 |

The Age of Reason:
A Scientific Revolution
AD 1600

OVERVIEW ❖ OVERVIEW ❖ OVERVIEW ❖ OVERVIEW ❖ OVERVIEW

In the years that spanned the lives of Galileo and Newton, science and philosophy flowered in Europe. Discoveries about the nature of the universe and technological breakthroughs led to far-reaching changes, including the Industrial Revolution.

A century of genius

The ideas of the Renaissance had by the seventeenth century spread throughout Europe. People questioned what they were now able to read in the Bible. They also questioned what they found in the classical philosophers' accounts of the world. People began to assume the right to think things through for themselves. Bertrand Russell called it 'a century of genius'.

Galileo's observations of the cosmos were part of this movement. By 1700, craftsmen had built the first orrery, a working model of the solar system operated by turning a handle. The universe was a machine.

A growing interest in human anatomy led to more dissections; previously the Church had been strong enough to forbid dissection. The work of the anatomists led to important discoveries about the way the human body worked. In 1628 an English doctor, William Harvey (1578–1657), discovered that blood circulates round the body consistently in one direction,

An orrery, used to represent the movements of the solar system.

| TIME LINE | 40,000BC | 10,000 | 5000 | 4000 | 500 | AD1 | 200 | 4 |

by way of arteries and veins. Science became increasingly experimental. Francis Bacon wrote, 'Nature, like a witness, reveals her secrets when put to torture.'

The need to dig deeper mines prompted the invention of more effective pumps, which led to Otto van Guericke's (1601–86) invention of an air pump, the research into gases of Robert Boyle (1627–91) and even Harvey's interpretation of the human heart as a pump. The invention of new machines led scientists to think of the universe itself in mechanical rather than religious terms.

It was Rene Descartes (1596–1650) who formulated the clearest statement about the Age of Reason. Only ideas which could be proved by evidence or by reasoning were true. All other ideas were to be mistrusted. This amounts to a definition of modern science.

Scholars began to gather together to exchange ideas and publish their work in journals. One of the first scientific societies was the Roman Academia dei Lincei founded in 1601. The Royal Society was founded in London in 1660. Six years later the Royal Academy was founded in Paris. By 1700 the Scientific Revolution was complete.

William Harvey discovered that blood circulated round the body in one direction.

CHRONOLOGY OF EVENTS
AD 1628 – 1666

1628
William Harvey, who discovered the circulation of the blood by way of arteries and veins, is born.

1700
The first orrery, a working model of the solar system, is made at about this time.

1601
Otto van Guericke, who invented an air pump, is born.

1601
The Roman Academia dei Lincei, one of the first scientific societies in the world, is founded.

1627
Robert Boyle is born.

1596
Rene Descartes is born.

1660
The Royal Society is founded in London

1666
The Royal Academy is founded in Paris.

Newton:
a New Vision of the Universe
AD 1642

The scientific discoveries of the seventeenth century led to many technological inventions, which in turn led to further discoveries and made possible the Industrial Revolution. The work of Isaac Newton prepared the way for this leap forward in the eighteenth century – and for the rocket science of the twentieth century.

Isaac Newton (1642–1727) was the greatest scientist of all time. In some ways he was a symbol of the Age of Reason, yet because he was prepared to challenge and investigate everything from scratch he repeatedly pushed his own mind to the limit – and sometimes beyond. At one point he suffered a serious mental breakdown.

Newton was an experimenter as well as a mathematician. He built a small steam engine on wheels to prove a law of motion. In 1665 he invented calculus (which he called 'fluxions'). It was also in 1665 that he watched an apple fall in his garden and began to formulate his theory of gravitation. The following year he measured the Moon's orbit, a key dimension in his theory, since he believed the Moon was kept in its orbit round the Earth by gravity.

Sir Isaac Newton, mathematician and physicist, 1642–1727.

TIME LINE	40,000BC	10,000	5000	4000	500	AD1	200	40

Sir Isaac Newton's reflecting telescope.

CHRONOLOGY OF EVENTS
AD 1642 – 1727

1642

Isaac Newton is born.

1665

Newton invents calculus (which he calls 'fluxions') and begins to formulate his theory of gravitation.

1666

Newton measures the Moon's orbit, a key dimension in his theory.

1668

Newton invents the reflecting telescope.

1672

Newton discovers that white light is made up of all the colours of the rainbow.

1684

Newton's gravitation theory is published.

1687

Principia Mathematica is published.

1689

Newton lunches with William III.

1727

Isaac Newton dies.

Newton's interest then turned to optics. In 1668 he invented the reflecting telescope, which became the standard type of telescope until the twentieth century and is still in use. It uses a curving mirror to correct and sharpen the fuzzy coloured-edged images seen through early 'Galilean' telescopes. Through simple experiments with prisms, he discovered that white light is made up of all the colours of the rainbow (1672).

After his gravitation theory was published in 1684, Edmond Halley approached him to write the epic work explaining the universe that was to make him into a celebrity, the *Principia Mathematica*. Halley himself paid to have it published in 1687.

Newton's major work was already over, the explanation of the universe on which most subsequent astronomy and physics have been based. After that he wasted a great deal of time on alchemy. He was a difficult, aggressive man with many admirers and few friends. But the recluse became a celebrity. When William III, another unpopular man, became king in 1689, his first request was to lunch with Isaac Newton the next day.

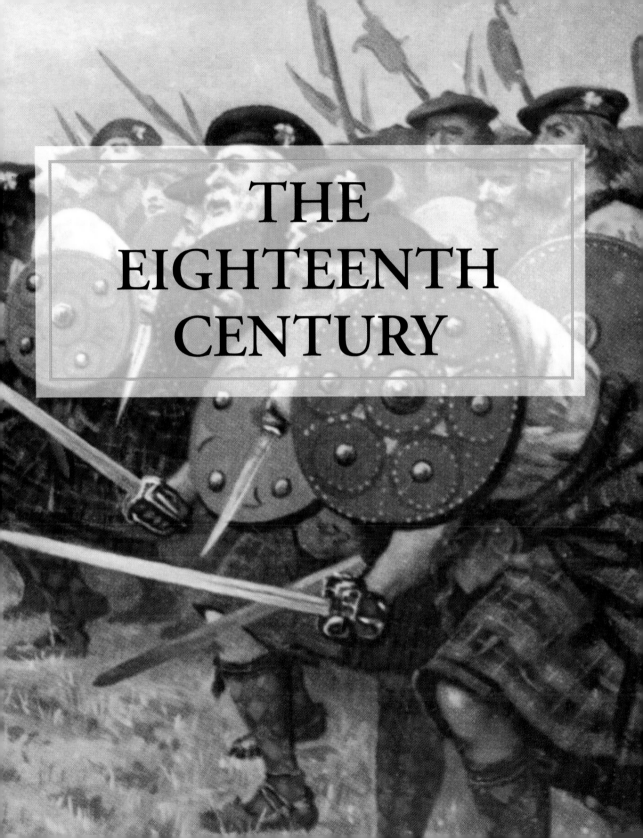

THE
EIGHTEENTH
CENTURY

The Industrial Revolution

AD 1700

OVERVIEW ❖ OVERVIEW ❖ OVERVIEW ❖ OVERVIEW ❖ OVERVIEW

Deforestation in Britain created the need to devise new industrial processes using coal rather than charcoal, and invent more effective pumps to drain coal mines that were penetrating deeper and deeper underground. The invention of the steam engine transformed many processes from cottage industries into factory industries. The growth of factories led directly to the growth of towns.

Steam power

The driving forces behind the Industrial Revolution were steam power and the depletion of English forests. As wood became scarcer, more coal was needed, and mines had to penetrate deeper underground, far below the water table. More effective pumps were needed to empty water out of the mines. The steam engine was developed, initially, by Thomas Newcomen (1712) to power these pumps; then other applications were found for it.

James Watt's more efficient steam engine (1775) was used in factories throughout Britain. It enabled tasks traditionally done by hand (spinning and weaving) to be done much faster. The first multi-reel spinning machine, the Spinning Jenny, was invented by

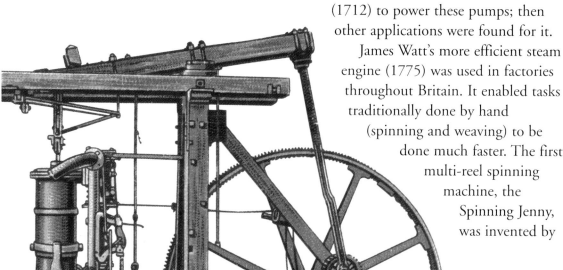

James Watt's steam engine, circa 1775.

TIME LINE	40,000BC	10,000	5000	4000	500	AD1	200	40

James Hargreaves (1764). It was initially hand-operated, but soon harnessed to a steam engine. John Kay's flying shuttle (1773) doubled the weaver's output; Edmund Cartwright's power loom (1790) further increased the speed of weaving.

The growth of towns

Many people were needed to work the machines and, because they needed to live within walking distance of the factories, thousands of people were drawn from the countryside into the towns to work. Living conditions in the countryside were very poor. The cottages were small and damp, there was a limited choice of jobs, most of them outdoor and all-weather and wages were very low. The factories were noisy and dangerous, but at least clean and dry. The growth of towns was a major side-effect of the Industrial Revolution.

The shortage of wood meant that charcoal could no longer be used for smelting iron. Abraham Darby invented a method of smelting using roasted coal (coke) and this paved the way for the mass production of iron, which was needed to build the many new machines.

The new factories and new machines were paid for largely with money earned from British colonies - not least from the slave trade; there were lots of rich merchants who had capital to invest. Peace and huge reserves of coal also helped Britain to lead the Industrial Revolution, which gradually spread to other European countries.

CHRONOLOGY OF EVENTS
AD 1712 – 1835

1712

Thomas Newcomen develops a steam engine to power pumps that will drain mines.

1775

James Watt invents a more efficient steam engine.

1764

James Hargreaves invents the Spinning Jenny, the first multi-reel spinning machine (patented in 1770).

1769

Richard Arkwright develops a water-powered spinning frame.

1773

John Kay's flying shuttle is invented.

1785

The power loom is invented by Edmund Cartwright.

1835

England is now producing over 60 percent of the world's cotton goods.

The Agricultural Revolution

AD 1700

OVERVIEW ❖ OVERVIEW ❖ OVERVIEW ❖ OVERVIEW ❖ OVERVIEW

In lowland Europe, landowners enclosed the communal open fields and started experimenting with crop rotations. These created food surpluses, profits and the desire to make further improvements. The Agricultural Revolution had a negative side – the displacement of poor people from the countryside and the weakening of village life.

Enclosure

European farming methods remained unchanged for hundreds of years. It was only in the sixteenth century that significant change began, when landowners started forcing poor people out of their homes, off the medieval open fields, so that the land could be enclosed. The old open fields – often three or four surrounding each village – were criss-crossed by stone walls, earth banks, fences or hedges, transforming the landscape of much of lowland Europe.

The creation of large enclosed fields under private ownership allowed farmers to experiment with crop rotations (wheat in the first year, turnips in the second, barley in the third, clover in the fourth). This rotation left out the traditional completely unproductive fallow year. Clover put nutrients back into the soil, restoring its fertility. A pioneer in crop rotation was the politician Charles 'Turnip' Townshend (1674–1738).

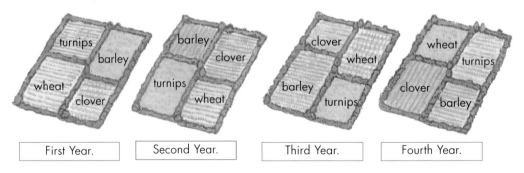

First Year.   Second Year.   Third Year.   Fourth Year.

TIME LINE	40,000BC	10,000	5000	4000	500	AD1	200	4

The old medieval three-field system had been a satisfactory subsistence system, producing just enough food for the villagers to eat. The new system allowed for population growth and produced a surplus that could be sold, often to people in the growing towns and cities. This shift from subsistence to commercial farming was the rural equivalent of the Industrial Revolution in the towns.

As farm profits grew, progressive farmers experimented with new methods. Thomas Coke, Earl of Leicester, encouraged selective breeding of sheep and cattle on his farms. Within a few years, significantly improved breeds had been developed. Coke held annual conferences at his house, Holkham Hall, where landowners from all over Europe were invited to discuss and exchange new ideas in farming.

The disinherited poor

The negative side of these improvements was the eviction of the poor, who drifted into the towns in increasing numbers, from the early sixteenth century onwards. In England, these unfortunate people were called vagabonds and they were treated with little consideration. As village populations shrank, village life with all the folk traditions that had gone on for centuries began to weaken. Huge social changes were underway in both town and country.

CHRONOLOGY OF EVENTS
AD 1644 – 1770

1644
Sir Richard Weston (a Royalist fugitive) brings the Flemish idea of crop rotation back to England.

1720
Jethro Tull pioneers the rotation of crops, which makes fallowing unnecessary.

1730
Charles 'Turnip' Townshend retires from politics to refine Jethro Tull's crop rotation.

1733
Jethro Tull publishes *The Horse-Hoing Husbandry*. Tull also invents a seed drill. He pioneers the technique for sowing in rows, which facilitates weeding.

1759
The first Enclosure Acts are passed in England, enabling common land to be enclosed.

1770
Robert Bakewell experiments with selective breeding; by inbreeding he produces a new breed of sheep, the Leicesters.

The Jacobite Rebellion

AD 1715

OVERVIEW ❖ OVERVIEW ❖ OVERVIEW ❖ OVERVIEW ❖ OVERVIEW

When George I became king of the recently United Kingdom, many people, especially Scottish Catholics, felt that James II's son James Stuart had a superior claim. Two Jacobite rebellions were mounted, in 1715 and 1745, to try to reinstate the Stuart royal family. The English establishment put down this move to topple the Protestant Hanoverian dynasty with great severity and cruelty.

Jacobite victory at the Battle of Prestonpans, 1745.

The 'Fifteen' Rebellion

When Queen Anne died leaving no surviving children in 1714, the Act of Settlement (1701) dictated that the British crown should go to the Protestant descendants of James I. Anne's brother, George of Hanover, a Protestant great-grandson of James I, became king. Some people thought James Stuart, a great-grandson of James I and the son of the more recent

TIME LINE	40,000BC	10,000	5000	4000	500	AD1	200	4

monarch James II, had a better claim. The Scots supported him because they were unhappy about the recent forced Union with England to make a 'United Kingdom' in 1707.

The supporters of Prince James Francis Stuart (1688–1766), then living in France and known as the Old Pretender, were known as Jacobites. A Jacobite army landed in 1715 and fought two battles against the English. At Sheriffmuir, 12,000 Jacobites led by the Earl of Mar were defeated by 4,000 English soldiers led by the Duke of Argyll. The Jacobite army was finally defeated at Preston in Lancashire. James Stuart himself arrived in Scotland in December 1715, sensed that support was weakening, and fled back to France.

The 'Forty-Five' Rebellion

In 1745, James's son, Charles Edward Stuart (1720–1788), known as 'Bonnie Prince Charlie' or the Young Pretender, led another rising. Initially he was successful and he began a long march south to take London. At Derby, he realised that English Catholics were not joining his army as he had hoped. He lost his nerve and turned back.

Early in 1746, the Jacobite army was massacred at the Battle of Culloden. Bonnie Prince Charlie escaped from the battlefield and made his way to the Hebrides. After a few months in hiding he managed to escape disguised as the maid of Flora Macdonald (1722–1790).

Reprisals were harsh, to prevent any recurrence. Many Highland clan chiefs were executed, the clans were forbidden to carry weapons or wear tartan or play bagpipes. The Highland clearances began: the systematic emptying of the Scottish Highlands.

CHRONOLOGY OF EVENTS
AD 1715 – 1746

1715

The 'Fifteen' Rebellion. A Jacobite army lands in Scotland in support of James Stuart, son of James II.

13 Nov 1715

Battle of Sheriffmuir.
The Jacobites are defeated.

5 Feb 1716

James Stuart senses that support is weakening, and returns to France.

25 July 1745

James's son, Charles Edward Stuart, lands in the Hebrides to lead another Jacobite rising.

2 Sep 1745

Battle of Prestonpans. The Jacobites win.

16 Apr 1746

Battle of Culloden The Jacobite army is massacred by British troops under the Duke of Cumberland.

20 Sep 1746

Prince Charles Edward escapes to France.

The Arts

AD 1700

OVERVIEW ❖ OVERVIEW ❖ OVERVIEW ❖ OVERVIEW ❖ OVERVIEW

There were extraordinary developments in the arts in both East and West. In Europe, the novel and the opera were developed into more substantial forms, and the first Romantic poetry was written, with its strong subjective tone and its interest in nature. Paintings were mainly decorative, while musical genius flowered as in no other century.

The Wave, by Katsushika Hokusai (1760-1849).

The visual arts

There were extraordinary developments in all of the arts. In Japan, woodblock printing advanced and composing haiku poetry became popular. Perhaps the most famous Japanese art work is *The Wave*, a beautiful print by Hokusai (died 1848). In China jade carving reached new heights, as did porcelain manufacture. European factories such as the Meissen factory near Dresden tried to imitate Chinese porcelain techniques. A pretty decorativeness was the hallmark of many paintings by Canaletto, Boucher, Fragonard and Watteau. In Goya, Joseph Wright and Hogarth there was a more down-to-earth quality.

Literature

In literature there were significant developments. The first novels were written. Ambitious dramas were written, such as Goethe's *Faust* (begun 1775, published 1808 and 1832) and

| TIME LINE | 40,000BC | 10,000 | 5000 | 4000 | 500 | AD 1 | 200 | 4 |

Schiller's *Die Rauber* (1782). Neoclassical poets tried for high-flown elegance. At the end of the century, Romantic poets Samuel Taylor Coleridge and William Wordsworth (1770–1850) wrote in a raw, emotional style that was intensely personal.

Silhouette of Wolfgang Amadeus Mozart at the piano.

Music

Great advances were made in music. Johann Sebastian Bach (1685–1750) was the outstanding composer of the first half of the eighteenth century. His *Six Brandenburg Concertos* date from 1721 and the *St Matthew Passion* from 1729.

Opera as an art form developed enormously, with more emphasis on plot and character development. Wolfgang Amadeus Mozart (1756–1791) was the most famous and influential composer of the later eighteenth century, writing operas such as *The Marriage of Figaro* and *The Magic Flute*. He wrote 41 outstanding symphonies. Mozart was a child prodigy, composing at 5, but dying at the tragically early age of 36.

The stature of Bach and Mozart overshadowed many other fine composers, such as Scarlatti (1685–1757), Vivaldi (1678–1741), Rameau (1683–1764) and Haydn (1732–1809).

CHRONOLOGY OF EVENTS
AD 1721 – 1798

1721
Bach: *Six Brandenburg Concertos.*

1725
Vivaldi: *The Four Seasons.*

1729
Bach: *St Matthew Passion.*

1756
Mozart is born.

1757
Scarlatti dies, after writing over 600 harpsichord sonatas.

1773
Mozart: *Symphonies 23-29.*

1775
Goethe: *Faust.*

1782
Schiller: *Die Rauber.*

1789
Mozart: *Don Giovanni.*

1790
Haydn: *Symphony No 104.*

1791
Mozart: *The Magic Flute.*

1798
Coleridge: *Rime of the Ancient Mariner.*

1798
Wordsworth: *Tintern Abbey.*

The Decline & Fall of the Mogul Empire
AD 1707

OVERVIEW ❖ OVERVIEW ❖ OVERVIEW ❖ OVERVIEW ❖ OVERVIEW

During the seventeenth and eighteenth centuries, the Mogul empire first grew to engulf most of the Indian subcontinent, then crumbled away, partly as a result of in-fighting among the Indian rulers and a Persian invasion, but mainly due to British determination to take India.

Decline of the empire

When Akbar, the founder of the Mogul empire, died in 1605, he was succeeded by his son Jahangir, who spent his time and wealth creating splendid buildings and gardens while his wife ruled. Shah Jahan (1592–1666) succeeded Jahangir in 1627, enlarging the empire to include the Deccan. He fell ill and his sons fought over the succession. One of the sons, Aurangzeb (1618–1707), killed his three brothers, imprisoned his father and seized the throne. Shah Jahan died in captivity and was buried next to his wife, Mumtaz Mahal, in the Taj Mahal, the beautiful white mausoleum which was built specially for her.

The Taj Mahal, mausoleum of the mogul Empress Mumtaz Mahal and her husband, its creator, Shah Jahan.

TIME LINE	40,000BC	10,000	5000	4000	500	AD1	200	4

Aurangzeb was the last of the great Mogul emperors. He conquered most of the rest of India, but was unable to conquer the Marathas of the north-west.

Collapse

After Aurangzeb died in 1707, the empire started to disintegrate. Local rulers fought to build up their own kingdoms, undermining the Mogul emperors. In western India and the Punjab, Sikh princes and Marathas organized rebellions. In 1739 the Persians under Nadir Shah attacked Delhi, the Mogul capital, and killed 30,000 inhabitants.

The Mogul empire was fatally undermined by European interference. The British were all the more determined to have India after losing the East Indies to the Dutch. The French and the British acquired huge areas in India, partly by brute force, partly by playing local rulers off against one another. At the Battle of Plassey near Calcutta in 1757, 3,200 soldiers led by Robert Clive (1725–74), an East India Company official, defeated 50,000 Indian and French troops. By 1763, Britain controlled the rich province of Bengal – now Bangladesh – and the whole of the east coast of India. India was by now in chaos, largely created by the British. The end of Mogul power came to an end finally when the British took the capital, Delhi, in 1803.

1605

Akbar, founder of the Mogul empire, dies and is succeeded by his son Jahangir.

1627

Shah Jahan succeeds Jahangir.

1657

Shah Jahan falls ill and his sons fight over the succession.

1658

One of the sons, Aurangzeb, imprisons his father and seizes the throne.

1666

Shah Jahan dies in captivity and is buried in the Taj Mahal.

1707

Aurangzeb dies.

1739

The Persians under Nadir Shah attack Delhi.

1757

Battle of Plassey near Calcutta. British soldiers led by Robert Clive defeat 50,000 Indian and French troops.

1763

Britain controls the rich province of Bengal – now Bangladesh – and the whole of the east coast of India.

1803

The end of Mogul power: the British take the capital, Delhi.

The Struggle for North America
AD 1759

OVERVIEW ❖ OVERVIEW ❖ OVERVIEW ❖ OVERVIEW ❖ OVERVIEW

Competition for colonies in eastern North America led to open conflict between Britain and France, in a series of small wars. This conflict culminated in a series of British victories, in which Quebec and Montreal were taken in 1759 and 1760. North America was established as a mainly British sphere of influence.

John Dee and the British Empire

The Spanish were the first Europeans to begin serious colonization of North America, following the Columbus voyages. It was Dr John Dee, Elizabeth I's magician, who suggested that England might found colonies in North America. He reminded the Queen that, not being Catholic, England was not bound by the Pope's division of the New World into Spanish and Portuguese spheres. A 'British Empire' might be created there. The first English colonies were founded along the Eastern Seaboard. The French aspired to colonies and penetrated inland up the St Lawrence and Mississippi, occupying a great swathe of North America to the west of the English. The Spanish occupied Florida.

Power struggle

Inevitably a power struggle broke out. There was fighting between French and British colonists in the seventeenth and eighteenth centuries: King William's War (1689–97), Queen Anne's War (1702–13) and King George's War (1744–48). The fighting was sometimes sparked by local competition for land, but there was a higher-level power struggle going on between England and France too.

Fighting between the English and French broke out again in 1754, and back in Europe this became one of the issues in the Seven Years' War, which began in 1756. The French invaded the Ohio valley, which the British claimed. The French refused to leave. The fighting that ensued spread north into Canada. The French won victories at Fort Duquesne

TIME LINE	40,000BC	10,000	5000	4000	500	AD1	200	40(

Quebec captured: British troops scale the Heights of Abraham.

1493

Pope Alexander VI establishes a demarcation line between Spanish and Portuguese spheres of influence. The Spanish are given North America.

1577

Dr John Dee, Elizabeth I's magician, proposes that the Queen should challenge the Spanish claim and create her own 'British Empire'.

1584

The first English colony in North America is founded on Roanoake Island.

1754

Fighting between the English and French breaks out again in North America.

1756

In Europe the Seven Years' War begins.

1759

The British take Quebec.

1760

The British take Montreal. The generals on both sides are killed - Wolfe and Montcalm.

1791

The British Constitutional Act divides Quebec into two colonies, English-speaking Upper Canada and French-speaking Lower Canada.

(1755) and Fort Oswego (1756). The British won victories at Acadia (1755), Quebec (1759) and Montreal (1760). The British took Quebec by climbing up onto the Heights of Abraham, overlooking the city; the generals on both sides were killed during the battle – James Wolfe and the Marquis de Montcalm.

Overall the British were victorious, gaining many of the French colonies.

The British Constitutional Act of 1791 divided Quebec into two colonies, Upper Canada, which was English-speaking, and Lower Canada, where French was spoken. North America was now firmly established as a British sphere of influence.

Communications:
Canals, Balloons, Metalled Roads
AD 1700

OVERVIEW ❖ OVERVIEW ❖ OVERVIEW ❖ OVERVIEW ❖ OVERVIEW

Increasing trade and the expansion of industry meant that transport had to be revolutionized. Canals were built to move bulky raw materials to the factories. Roads were improved to make it easier to get goods to market. Telegraph systems using semaphore towers were devised to send messages quickly.

Growth of Industry and Communications

Increasing trade meant that transport too needed revolutionizing. The huge quantities of raw materials needed for the factories had to be transported as cheaply as possible. The manufactured goods had to be transported to the markets in the new cities and overseas.

There were other reasons why communications needed to improve. One was war.

Canals

Canals were built throughout Europe. Canal transport was cheap. Barges laden with coal and other raw materials were drawn by horses walking along tow-paths.

A barge on a French canal

The expansion of industry meant an expansion of business contacts, so transporting people also needed to become more efficient and reliable.

Metalled roads

The need to move goods to market and allow people to travel all the year round on business led to a transport

152

TIME LINE	40,000BC	10,000	5000	4000	500	AD1	200	400

Montgolfier's first air balloon, unmanned, was launched at Annonay and rose to 2000 metres. The Academie Royale des Sciences paid for the venture.

revolution: the development of metalled roads. John McAdam (1756–1836) made a fortune in New York before returning to his native Scotland in 1783 to began experimenting with road-construction. He remade the roads for the Bristol Turnpike Trust according his new method, using crushed stone, and raised to improve drainage. The first modern tarmacadam roads were laid in 1819.

Flight

The first experiments with flight began in the eighteenth century. An airship was designed but its designer died before it could be built. The Montgolfier brothers were pioneers in flying hot-air balloons; their first successful flight was a 9km journey over Paris in 1783. In 1785, the first flight across the English Channel by balloon was made.

Sending messages

From 1794 onwards, coded messages could be sent using semaphore. This was done using large, movable metal arms mounted on the tops of towers. The signals could be seen through telescopes from many miles away, so a network of towers could be used to telegraph messages rapidly across country. This system was in use in the Napoleonic Wars. In 1804, the first electric telegraph was successfully demonstrated in Spain.

CHRONOLOGY OF EVENTS
AD 1681 – 1804

1681
Canal du Midi, connecting Mediterranean with Bay of Biscay, is completed.

1761
Bridgewater Canal, connecting Worsley mines to Manchester, is engineered by James Brindley.

1783
John McAdam begins experimenting with road-construction in Scotland.

1819
The first modern tarmacadam roads are laid.

1783
The first successful flight by balloon, a 9km journey over Paris, is made.

1785
The first flight across the English Channel by balloon (Francois Blanchard and John Jeffries).

1794
Semaphore is introduced, enabling coded messages to be sent.

1804
The first electric telegraph is successfully demonstrated in Spain.

The Enlightenment

AD 1700

OVERVIEW ❖ OVERVIEW ❖ OVERVIEW ❖ OVERVIEW ❖ OVERVIEW

In the eighteenth century many scholars and writers believed they had woken up to new insights, free of ideas from the past. Advances were made in science, new scientific societies were formed, people met in Parisian salons, and new ideas of political freedom were in the air, in both France and America.

ENCYCLOPÉDIE,

OU

DICTIONNAIRE RAISONNÉ

DES SCIENCES,

DES ARTS ET DES MÉTIERS,

PAR UNE SOCIÉTÉ DE GENS DE LETTRES.

Mis en ordre & publié par M. *DIDEROT*, de l'Académie Royale des Sciences & des Belles-Lettres de Prusse; &, quant à la PARTIE MATHÉMATIQUE, par M. *D'ALEMBERT*, de l'Académie Royale des Sciences de Paris, de celle de Prusse, & de la Société Royale de Londres.

Tantùm series juncturaque pollet,
Tantùm de medio sumptis accedit honoris! HORAT.

TOME PREMIER.

A PARIS,

Chez {
BRIASSON, *rue Saint Jacques, à la Science.*
DAVID l'aîné, *rue Saint Jacques, à la Plume d'or.*
LE BRETON, Imprimeur ordinaire du Roy, *rue de la Harpe.*
DURAND, *rue Saint Jacques, à Saint Landry, & au Griffon.*

M. DCC. LI.

AVEC APPROBATION ET PRIVILÉGE DU ROY.

Frontispiece to *The Encyclopedia of Science, Art and Engineering* by Denis Diderot (1713–84) published in Paris, 1751.

Eighteenth century scholars, artists and writers believed they had new insights, either by depending on the power of reason or by depending on personal revelation. They felt themselves freed from the ideas, religious beliefs and superstitions of the past. Newton's optical experiments were part of this. This was the time when modern chemistry began and significant advances were made in biology and archaeology, with both Thomas Jefferson in America and William Stukeley in England taking very different new approaches to the distant past.

One remarkable product of the Enlightenment was Denis Diderot's *Encyclopedia*, published between 1751 and 1772. This 28-volume work, with text and many illustrations, was a compilation of articles by experts on many different subjects, explaining modern scientific discoveries. The *Encyclopedia* was, even so, subject to censorship by Diderot's publisher.

Other major figures at this time were the Scottish economist Adam Smith, the French philosophers Voltaire and Jean-Jacques Rousseau (1712–78).

TIME LINE	40,000BC	10,000	5000	4000	500	AD1	200	4

François Marie Arouet, Voltaire, (1694–1778).

Voltaire (1694–1778) was the most famous French writer of his time, producing philosophical works, plays and the novel, *Candide*. In France, the ideas of Voltaire and Rousseau on government began to have an effect on the political climate, and led eventually to the French Revolution. Another revolutionary thinker was the English Tom Paine (1737–1809), who wrote a book entitled *The Rights of Man*. In it he saw 'a dawn of reason rising on the world'. The Enlightenment spread to America, where Benjamin Franklin (1706–90) in 1743 founded the first scientific society in the New World, the American Philosophical Society in Philadelphia. New ideas of political freedom were in the air in both France and America.

Well-educated men and women met in the drawing rooms of noble ladies, who saw themselves as patrons of the arts and sciences; in these settings, there were informal discussions and formal lectures. Madame Geoffrin's salon was famous for its gatherings of Parisian philosophers.

CHRONOLOGY OF EVENTS
AD 1724 – 1796

1724

William Stukeley: *Itinerarium Curiosum* (discovering British antiquities).

1749

Benjamin Franklin founds the American Philosophical Society.

1751

Denis Diderot: *Encyclopedia (Part 1)*.

1759

Voltaire: *Candide*.

1762

Rousseau: *Social Contract* and *Emile*.

1772

Denis Diderot's 28-volume *Encyclopedia* is completed.

1776

Tom Paine: *Common Sense*
Thomas Jefferson: *Declaration of Independence*.

1786

Tom Paine: *Dissertations on Government*.

1792

Tom Paine: *The Rights of Man*.

1796

Tom Paine: *The Age of Reason (Part 2)*.

Romanticism

AD 1770

OVERVIEW ❖ OVERVIEW ❖ OVERVIEW ❖ OVERVIEW ❖ OVERVIEW

Romanticism was a powerful popular movement in all the arts. It emphasized the individual imagination of the artist, the power of emotion, the importance of heroes, and led to a revival of nationalism. Above all it produced great art – the paintings of Turner, the operas of Wagner, the poems of Keats, the novels of Melville, the visions of Blake.

The nature of Romanticism

Romanticism was widespread in origins and influence, and it had greater reach and staying power than any other artistic and intellectual movement in the last 500 years. It began in England and Germany in the 1770s, swept through Europe by 1820, and in music at least circled the world.

Romanticism was a reaction to the Enlightenment, emphasizing the personal, imaginative and visionary side. It brought with it a deeper appreciation of the beauty of nature, a heightened examination of human personality, and a new preoccupation with the genius and the hero. The artist was a supremely individual creator with all kinds of inner struggles. There was a new interest in folk culture and the medieval, and a consequent revival of nationalism.

Norham Castle on the River Tweed, Summer's Morn, Turner, 1837.

Literature and art

English romanticism dates from Wordsworth and Coleridge's *Lyrical Ballads* (1798) and the poetry of Byron (1788–1824), Shelley (1792–1822) and Keats (1795–1821), which focused on the poet's personal reaction to life.

Blake (1757–1827) searched for the spiritual reality underlying the physical in poems and images that were equally arresting. The new appreciation of nature flowered in the paintings of Constable (1776–1837) and Turner (1775–1851).

Romanticism in German literature was represented by Lessing, Holderlin, Schiller and most of all Goethe (1749–1832). French Romanticism was championed by Victor Hugo (1802–1885). Other French writers include Lamartine, de Vigny, George Sand and Dumas pere. In Russia there were Pushkin and Lermontov.

Romanticism spread to the New World in the work of Emerson, Poe, Longfellow and Whitman (1819–1891), and the novels of Hawthorne and Melville (also 1819–1891).

Romanticism in music

Romanticism in music first appeared as a powerful image of untamed natural forces, in the central anti-hero of Mozart's *Don Giovanni* (1787). Subjective emotion found expression through melody (in Schumann's lieder), the hankering for the past through the use of folk idioms (in Dvorak's symphonies). Often linked with nationalism, the movement reached a climax in the operas of Richard Wagner (1813–1883). After that, Romanticism became luxuriously elegiac, as in the music of Mahler (1860–1911) and Rachmaninov (1873–1943), before petering out in Hollywood film music.

Die Walkure, Wagner.
Agnes Borgo as Brunnhilde, at the Paris Opera.

The Voyages of Captain Cook: Australia & the Pacific
AD 1768

OVERVIEW ❖ OVERVIEW ❖ OVERVIEW ❖ OVERVIEW ❖ OVERVIEW

The Dutch discovered the west coast of Australia, the islands of Tasmania and New Zealand, but showed no interest in colonizing them. The three voyages of Captain Cook established the east coast of Australia and the emptiness of the South Pacific.

The Dutch explorers

Dutch merchantmen sailing across the Indian Ocean to the East Indies discovered the western shore of Australia by the 1620s, naming it New Holland. The size and shape of Australia remained unknown and many thought it was part of the great Southern Continent that for some reason was assumed to straddle the South Pole.

In 1642, Abel Tasman (c. 1603–59), a Dutch navigator, sailed south-east from Mauritius, missing the southern part of Australia altogether, and discovered Tasmania. Tasman sailed on to the east and discovered the South Island of New Zealand before sailing north. He proved that Australia was an island, but the Dutch left it alone.

Captain Cook

Captain James Cook's voyages to Australasia and the Pacific (1768–79) were the first systematic exploration of this huge region. Cook looked

Captain James Cook, 1728–1779.

TIME LINE	40,000BC	10,000	5000	4000	500	AD1	200	4

Captain Cook is killed in Hawaii (Sandwich Islands) during a quarrel over a stolen boat.

after his sailors, giving them an improved diet that included milk, malt and orange juice. He also made astronomical observations of the southern stars.

Cook's first voyage (1768–71) crossed the South Pacific, proving there was no large landmass, circumnavigated New Zealand. Cook then sailed west, landed at Botany Bay on the east coast of Australia and claimed the unwanted land for Britain. The second voyage was an ambitious exploration of the South Pacific, in which he came close to discovering Antarctica but saw no sign of the great Southern Continent. The third voyage revisited the South Pacific and took in the coast of Chile. Cook turned back because of ice. He landed at Hawaii, where he was killed in a skirmish with the islanders.

The voyages of James Cook had a great impact in Europe, where a whole new world of the imagination was opened up. Europeans were excited by the exotic customs of the many different peoples that Cook and the French traveller, La Pelouse, encountered on their journeys.

CHRONOLOGY OF EVENTS
AD 1620 – 1779

1620s

Dutch merchantmen discover the western shore of Australia.

1642

Abel Tasman discovers Tasmania and the South Island of New Zealand.

1643

Tasman is sent to find the 'Great South Land' and discovers Tonga and Fiji.

1755

James Cook enters the navy.

1768—71

Captain James Cook's first voyage to observe the transit of Venus.

1770

Cook explores the east coast of Australia, claims it for Britain.

1772–75

Cook's second voyage, an ambitious exploration of the South Pacific.

1776–79

Cook's third voyage revisits the Pacific, exploring as far north as the Bering Strait.

1779

Cook lands at Hawaii, where he is killed in a skirmish.

The American War of Independence

AD 1775

OVERVIEW ❖ OVERVIEW ❖ OVERVIEW ❖ OVERVIEW ❖ OVERVIEW

The British government expected the American colonists to pay taxes to support the military defence of America, but after the dismantling of the French colonies in 1763 the English colonists thought they no longer needed the British soldiers. They resented the British taxes and fought a short and successful War of Independence.

After the threat from the French had been removed at the end of the Seven Years' War (1763), the English colonists in America felt they no longer had the support of England to defend them. They began to hanker for independence. The British government wanted to occupy and govern the old French territories. The occupying army cost a lot of money and the British tried to levy higher taxes on the Americans. The colonial assemblies protested that it was unfair for the British to tax Americans, as they had no say in the way the British government was run. It was 'taxation without representation'.

In December 1773, in a demonstration against the British taxes, colonists disguised as native North Americans boarded British ships in Boston harbour. They threw the cargoes of tea overboard.

In 1775 the American War of Independence started with British troops attacking American

The Boston Tea Party, December 16, 1773
Dressed as Native Americans, rebels throw tea into Boston Harbour as a demonstration against unfair taxes.

TIME LINE	40,000BC	10,000	5000	4000	500	AD1	200	40

The Declaration of Independence, 1776.

soldiers at the battle of Bunker Hill. The British were successful at first, but the Americans had the ultimate advantage of fighting on home territory. The British army surrendered at Yorktown in Virginia in 1781 following defeat by an American army under George Washington. The British recognized America's independence in 1783.

During the war the colonists, led by Thomas Jefferson (1743–1826) drew up the American Declaration of Independence. It read, 'We hold these truths to be self-evident, that they are created equal, that they are endowed with by their Creator certain inalienable rights, and among these are life, liberty and the pursuit of happiness.'.

The success of this fight for political liberty in America had a great effect in France, where revolution was not long in following. The American Constitution was accepted in 1789; it stated that America was to be a union and a democracy, but that each state would hold its own assembly.

CHRONOLOGY OF EVENTS
AD 1774 – 1783

20 Oct 1774

The Continental Congress decides to stop trading with Britain.

1775

The American War of Independence starts.

3 July 1775

George Washington takes command in Cambridge, Mass.

15 May 1776

The Virginia Convention proposes independence for the American colonies.

4 July 1776

The American Declaration of Independence is signed at Philadelphia.

19 Sep 1777

First Battle of Saratoga. Stalemate.

7 Oct 1777

Second Battle of Saratoga. General Gates (American) decisively defeats General Burgoyne (British).

19 Oct 1781

The British army surrenders at Yorktown in Virginia.

1783

Britain recognizes America's independence.

The French Revolution

AD 1789

OVERVIEW ❖ OVERVIEW ❖ OVERVIEW ❖ OVERVIEW ❖ OVERVIEW

Economic crisis and the maltreatment of ordinary people led to the French Revolution, in which mainly middle class revolutionaries overthrew the monarchy, executed the King and Queen, Louis XVI and Marie Antoinette, and set up a republic.

In the late eighteenth century, France was in crisis socially and economically. Ordinary people had a very low standard of living with few rights, while the clergy and aristocrats lived in luxury. There were food shortages, high prices and a government that had overspent its budget. The government could borrow money or raise taxes, but first the States-General had to be recalled, an ancient assembly that had not met for 175 years. Middle-class discontent turned the States-General into a National Assembly demanding reform. Louis XVI made the mistake of sending troops to break up the Assembly. When the people of Paris heard about this, they took to the streets, rebelling against the King and his government. There were riots throughout France.

On 14 July 1789, a mob attacked the Bastille, a Parisian fortress and prison that symbolized the oppression of the 'old regime'. The mob unlocked the cells, released the prisoners and went on to demolish the building. Louis XIV had chosen Versailles as a safe place outside Paris, but now a mob of Parisian women marched on Versailles, seized Louis XVI and his wife, Marie Antoinette, who was hated mainly for being Austrian, and took them back to Paris.

Execution of Louis XVI during the French Revolution, January 21, 1793.

TIME LINE	40,000BC	10,000	5000	4000	500	AD1	200	4

In 1791, the Assembly formed a new government. The royal family attempted to escape, and nearly succeeded, but their coach was stopped at Vincennes and they were imprisoned along with many other aristocrats. The new government wanted to purge France of the people who had ruined it, and as many as 40,000 people were sentenced to death. They were beheaded on the guillotine, Louis XVI and Marie Antoinette among them.

Governments of other European countries were afraid that the revolution would spread, and war was declared on the French republic. As more and more people were executed as 'enemies of the people' in the Reign of Terror (1793–4), fear spread through France. When the Reign of Terror ended in July 1794, with the execution of Robespierre, the Jacobin leader, there was general celebration. France would nevertheless never go back to the old-style absolutist monarchy with an over-privileged aristocracy and clergy.

CHRONOLOGY OF EVENTS
AD 1789 – 1794

14 July 1789

The fall of the Bastille.

4 Aug 1789

All feudal rights are abolished by the Assembly.

25 Jun 1791

Louis XVI and his family are arrested at Varennes while attempting to escape and imprisoned.

10 Aug 1792

The people of Paris storm the Tuileries Palace.

21 Sep 1792

The National Convention abolishes the monarchy.

21 Jan 1793

Louis XVI is beheaded.

16 Oct 1793

Marie Antoinette is guillotined.

March 1794

Robespierre defeats his rivals, sending Danton to the guillotine.

26 July 1794

Robespierre delivers a long harangue at the Convention.

27 Jul 1794

A conspiracy of moderates leads to Robespierre's arrest.

28 Jul 1794

Robespierre is guillotined. The Reign of Terror ends.

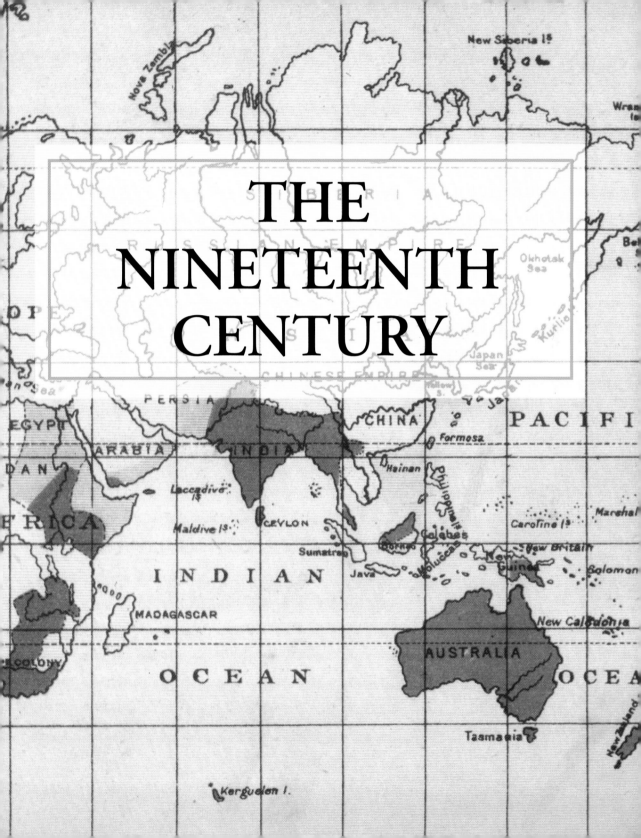

THE NINETEENTH CENTURY

Communications:
Steam Trains & Steamships
AD 1800

People were quick to realise the enormous potential of the steam engine for powered transport. At the beginning of the nineteenth century both steam locomotives to run along rails on land and steam ships to cross the sea were invented.

Steam trains

In 1803 Richard Trevithick invented a steam engine that powered a locomotive to pull wagons along a track in a coal mine. This was the very first steam train, and it ran for the first time in 1804. George Stephenson adapted the locomotive to pull passenger wagons. On 27 September 1825, the Stockton and Darlington Railway became the first public passenger railway in the world. The train that launched the railway age was hauled by Stephenson's aptly named Locomotive No. 1. By 1855, thousands of miles of track had spread across Britain; the great age of railway travel had begun.

Steamships

Small steamships using steam engines to power paddle wheels, like the 'Charlotte Dundas' (1801), were built early in the nineteenth century , but conservatism prevented the new ships from being exploited. They were used mainly as river boats on the Mississippi and were not regarded as suitable for long voyages on

The Rocket, built by George Stephenson in 1829.

TIME LINE	40,000BC	10,000	5000	4000	500	AD1	200	4(

the open sea. The first generation of steamships had masts and sails, just in case the engine failed. Many people believed that ships made of iron could not float. The first Atlantic crossing by steamship was made in 1819, but regular steamship crossings were not to come until the British and American Steam Navigation's 'Sirius' in 1834 and, within a few hours, the much larger 'Great Western'. Charles Dickens crossed the Atlantic in the 'Britannia' in 1842.

Isambard Kingdom Brunel's 'Great Britain' was launched in July 1843; she was the most advanced ship afloat, with an iron hull, screw propellers and a big sail area carried on six masts. When she ran onto rocks in Dundrum Bay in Ireland, and remained aground for almost a year without breaking up or sinking, people realised how strong iron ships were. In 1857 Brunel's 'Great Eastern', by far the most ambitious ship built up to that time, crossed the Atlantic. At 211 metres long, she was over twice the length of the 'Great Britain'. It became obvious, at last, that steamships could voyage anywhere, and services between Europe, South America and India were soon established.

CHRONOLOGY OF EVENTS
AD 1801 – 1857

1801

'Charlotte Dundas', the first steamship, is launched.

1803

Richard Trevithick invents a steam engine that powers a locomotive to pull wagons along a track.

1819

The first Atlantic crossing by steamship is made.

1829

Stephenson's *Rocket* wins the Liverpool and Manchester railway locomotive competition.

1834

Regular Atlantic steamship crossings begin – the 'Sirius' and the 'Great Western'.

1842

Charles Dickens crosses the Atlantic in the 'Britannia'.

1857

The 'Great Eastern' crosses the Atlantic.

Now part of the National Collection, the 9F 2-10-0, No. 92220, was one of the last main-line steam locomotives to be designed in Great Britain.

Napoleon & the Napoleonic Wars
AD 1799

OVERVIEW ❖ OVERVIEW ❖ OVERVIEW ❖ OVERVIEW ❖ OVERVIEW

A bold and imaginative general, Napoleon captured the French imagination and was able to seize power in 1799. He introduced many enlightened reforms in France, but his aggression abroad weakened both France and his own hold on power. He was finally defeated at Waterloo in 1815.

Napoleon Bonaparte (1769–1821), a Corsican, was an able soldier who made rapid progress through the ranks and was a general at the age of 26. His success in capturing northern Italy for France in 1797 made him dangerously popular as far as the French government, the Directory, were concerned. It was suggested that he should invade England, but Napoleon proposed invading Egypt instead, to sever Britain's trade route to India. This plan failed when Nelson destroyed the French fleet in 1798. Napoleon abruptly returned to France in 1799 and seized power in a characteristically bold way. He marched into the government buildings with

The Battle of Waterloo, June 18, 1815.
Napoleon among his men, facing defeat as the battle draws to a close: his carriage awaits to take him from the f

TIME LINE	40,000BC	10,000	5000	4000	500	AD1	200	40

his bodyguards, dismissed the Council of 500 and appointed three consuls to run France; he would be first consul.

Napoleon ruled France for 15 years, crowning himself emperor in 1804. Within France Napoleon made many reforms, including an improved system of education, a reorganized government and new laws.

Napoleon Bonaparte
1769–1821.

The aggressive military policy pursued against the rest of Europe was less constructive and caused enormous loss of life. He mustered a huge army of over two million. The continuing war with Britain, the fighting in central Europe (defeating Austria and Russia at Austerlitz in 1805), the Continental System (a trade blockade against Britain), the invasion of Spain in 1808 and the disastrous invasion of Russia in 1812 all weakened France and contributed to Napoleon's eventual downfall. The loss of Spain and Portugal made Napoleon particularly unpopular in France.

The British victory masterminded by Lord Nelson (1785–1805) at the Battle of Trafalgar in 1805 saved Britain from a French invasion. In 1813 Napoleon was defeated at Leipzig. In 1815 he made a brief return to power before being defeated at Waterloo by a combined Prussian and British army under Blucher and Wellington. After that he abdicated and was exiled to the remote island of St Helena in the South Atlantic, where he died (perhaps by poisoning) in 1821.

CHRONOLOGY OF EVENTS
AD 1769 – 1821

1769
Napoleon Bonaparte is born in Corsica.

1797
Napoleon captures northern Italy for France.

1798
Nelson destroys the French fleet.

1799
Napoleon dismisses the Council of 500 and seizes power. He is named 'first consul'.

1804
Napoleon crowns himself emperor.

1805
The Battle of Trafalgar saves Britain from a French invasion.

Oct 1813
Napoleon is defeated at Leipzig.

11 April 1814
Napoleon abdicates, and is exiled to Elba.

20 March 1815
Napoleon briefly returns to power.

18 June 1815
Battle of Waterloo, Napoleon's final defeat.

22 June 1815
Napoleon abdicates.

15 July 1815
Napoleon surrenders himself to Captain Maitland of the Bellerophon at Rochefort, and is exiled to St Helena.

5 May 1821
Napoleon dies.

Inventions:
Electricity & Photography
AD 1831

OVERVIEW ❖ OVERVIEW ❖ OVERVIEW ❖ OVERVIEW ❖ OVERVIEW

New inventions included the dynamo, which produced a steady electric current, electric lighting and hydro-electric power stations. It became possible to mass produce cheap steel, leading the way to more efficient ship design. Photography meant that people became better informed, and artists were released from 'realism'.

The second, nineteenth century, phase of the Industrial Revolution brought a spate of new inventions. The English scientist Michael Faraday (1791–1867) invented the dynamo in 1831, which produced the first steady electric current. This paved the way for the practical exploitation of electricity. Thomas Edison (1847–1931) pioneered the electric light bulb (1879), which was first used in 1880 to light a steamship. People were afraid of electric lights in public buildings because they thought the dazzling light would damage their eyes. By 1900, that resistance was fading and a few homes had electric lights, which were fixed to wall brackets like gas lamps.

Edison also invented the phonograph or gramophone in 1877. The music was recorded onto cylinders that had to be turned by hand, and amplified by a large horn. This made it possible for people to listen to music repeatedly and understand better how it worked.

The first hydro-electric power station was built in 1882. It made electricity cheaply out of the force of falling water, and would become popular in mountainous countries such as Norway and Switzerland.

In 1856 Henry Bessemer invented the steel converter, which enabled industrialists to mass produce

TIME LINE	40,000BC	10,000	5000	4000	500	AD1	200	40

A hydro-electric power station, using water to power huge turbines.

steel cheaply; steel was much stronger and more versatile than iron. The early iron ships were dangerously and inefficiently heavy, but steel hulls could be built much lighter; by 1900, most ships had steel hulls.

Another major industrial invention was a safe and manageable form of nitroglycerin called dynamite (1866). The Swedish chemist Alfred Nobel (1833–1896) invented the explosive to improve productivity in the mining industry, but it was to have far-reaching applications in the munitions industry too.

An invention that seemed harmless and relatively useless at first turned out to have huge social, artistic and educational implications – photography. The first photographs (daguerrotypes or 'photogenic drawings') were taken by Louis Daguerre and William Fox Talbot in 1838. The American Civil War was photographed. People could begin to see what war was like. Once George Eastman invented the first roll film camera (1888), anybody could take photographs. Artists were released from the obligation to paint 'realistic' pictures, and the way was clear for new types of art, impressionism, expressionism and abstract art, to develop.

CHRONOLOGY OF EVENTS
AD 1831 – 1888

1831
English scientist Michael Faraday invents the dynamo.

1838
Louis Daguerre and William Fox Talbot take the first photographs.

1856
Henry Bessemer invents the steel converter.

1866
Alfred Nobel invents dynamite.

1877
Thomas Edison invents the phonograph or gramophone.

1879
Edison pioneers the electric light bulb.

1880
Electric light bulbs are first used to light a steamship.

1882
The first hydro-electric power station is built.

1888
George Eastman invents the first roll film camera.

The End of Slavery

AD 1863

OVERVIEW ❖ OVERVIEW ❖ OVERVIEW ❖ OVERVIEW ❖ OVERVIEW

Rousseau's (1764) idea that 'Man is born free, but everywhere he is in chains' inspired the anti-slavery movement. Revolts by slaves in French colonies and American plantations were savagely suppressed. William Wilberforce succeeded in getting the slave trade banned throughout the British Empire in 1807, and this marked the beginning of the collapse of the slave trade. But slavery itself was not abolished in the USA until 1863.

Slave rebellion in the Caribbean

The French Revolution spread to the Caribbean in 1791, when the French National Assembly gave the vote to slaves in what is now Haiti. The plantation owners blocked the measure and the slaves rebelled, destroying houses and plantations, killing the owners. The rebellion was led by one of the slaves, Pierre Toussaint L'Ouverture (1743–1803), who declared himself ruler of Santo Domingo in 1801. French troops regained control in 1802; Toussaint was captured and taken to France where he died in prison in 1803. In that year slavery was made legal again in all the French colonies.

Rousseau and the Social Contract

France was growing rich on taxes on the produce of its colonies – and so were Spain and Britain. Much of this wealth was based on slave labour. As many as 15 million people were shipped across from Africa to the New World between 1450 and 1870. There were many in Europe who disliked the slave trade,

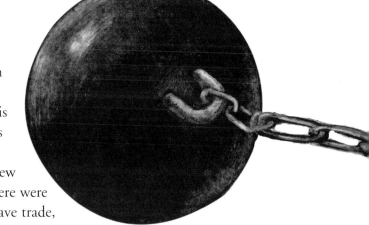

TIME LINE	40,000BC	10,000	5000	4000	500	AD1	200	40

but objections were swept aside as it was seen as the only economic way of running the plantations. The slaves were often treated harshly and cruelly by their owners, who whipped them if they did not work hard enough. A small number of Europeans campaigned on the slaves' behalf.

In 1764, Rousseau wrote in his Social Contract, 'Man is born free, but everywhere he is in chains,' inspiring the French and American Revolutions – and the anti-slavery campaign.

After a slave revolt in Virginia in 1831 repressive laws were passed by the southern states to keep the slaves in check.

William Wilberforce and the ending of slavery

In Britain, William Wilberforce (1759–1833) began his campaign against the slave trade in 1784. He succeeded in getting it made illegal throughout the British Empire in 1807 – a major step forward.

Serfdom ended in Russia in 1861. Slavery was not abolished in the USA, the 'Land of the Free', until after the American Civil War, in 1863.

1764

Rousseau's *Social Contract*: 'Man is born free, but everywhere he is in chains'.

1784

William Wilberforce begins his campaign against the slave trade.

1791

The French National Assembly gives the vote to slaves in what is now Haiti.

1807

The slave trade is banned throughout the British Empire.

1808

The importation of slaves into the USA is banned by Jefferson.

1831

Laws are passed by the southern states of the USA to keep the slaves in check.

1834

Slavery is abolished throughout the British Empire. On Emancipation Day (1 August), 750,000 slaves are freed.

1861

Serfdom ends in Russia.

1863

Slavery is abolished in the USA.

The Trail of Tears: the Plight of 'First Peoples' in America

AD 1800

OVERVIEW ❖ OVERVIEW ❖ OVERVIEW ❖ OVERVIEW ❖ OVERVIEW

The flood of Europeans arriving in America following independence created enormous pressure for land. Native North American peoples living on the Eastern Seaboard were forcibly moved west into the Prairies. Then the white settlers wanted the Prairies too. By the end of the nineteenth century, the Indian way of life had been virtually wiped out.

European settlers from many different countries flocked to America following the Declaration of Independence in 1776. Many of these people were poor and disadvantaged, and hoped to be able to make a better life for themselves. The population of America was 4 million in 1790; by 1830 it was 23 million and by 1880 50 million. This huge influx of people arrived through New York and to begin with most settled in the north-eastern states. As time passed, the immigrants moved south and west, crossing the Appalachian Mountains and reaching the Mississippi valley.

Large areas wanted for colonization by the white settlers were already occupied by Native North Americans. The Cherokee Indians' traditional homelands were in North Carolina and Georgia, land wanted by the US government for white settlement. The Cherokees were offered $5.7 million by the government to move out, but

New York Harbour.
Most immigrants into North America in the nineteenth century entered their new homeland through New York.

most refused. The government response was to send in troops to get them out by force. The Cherokees were driven west to settle on newly created reservations in the Prairies, which were dry with cold winters. The Creek, Seminole and Choctaw Indians were similarly forced to set off on the 'Trail of Tears' to the Prairies, a journey on which many died. Their unhappiness at being separated from their homelands, with which they felt a special bond, is hard for us to imagine.

The US government bought the Prairies, a huge area between the Mississippi and the Rockies, from the French in 1803. This transaction, called the Louisiana Purchase, doubled the size of the USA. Unfortunately, this land too was occupied by Native North Americans, but the government sold off much of it, without regard for the native peoples, to farmers and ranchers.

The disruption of the Native North American way of life continued through the nineteenth century. The killing of so many Native North Americans and the destruction of their way of life is seen by many as a crime against humanity.

CHRONOLOGY OF EVENTS
AD 1776 – 1890

1776

American Declaration of Independence. Start of large-scale European immigration.

1790

The population of America reaches 4 million.

1803

The Louisiana Purchase. The US government buys the Prairies from the French.

1830

The population of America reaches 23 million. The Indian Removal Act legalizes the displacement of Native North Americans.

1835

Cherokees in Georgia are offered $5.7 million by the government to move out, but most refuse.

1876

Battle of the Little Big Horn. US troops fail to drive the Indians off the Prairies and into their reservations.

1880

The population of America reaches 50 million.

1890

The Battle of Wounded Knee. US troops massacre 300 Sioux Indians in South Dakota, ending Indian resistance to white settlement in North America.

1848: a Year of Revolutions in Europe

AD 1848

OVERVIEW ❖ OVERVIEW ❖ OVERVIEW ❖ OVERVIEW ❖ OVERVIEW

Revolution broke out in many European countries in 1848. People were dissatisfied with the way they were governed, in particular with the lack of democracy. In Britain the Chartists failed, but in France the revolutionaries succeeded in replacing their monarch with a 'Prince-President', Napoleon's nephew. Nationalism was a driving force behind the revolutions in Germany and Italy.

In 1848, riots, revolts and full-scale revolutions broke out in many European countries. People were dissatisfied with their governments, and for the same reasons that lay behind the French Revolution 60 years earlier. Resentment at the way people were governed had been simmering since 1815, and there had been outbreaks of rebellion in the 1830s. The Enlightenment and the Romantic movement both played a part in making people think that they should have a greater say than the state in what happened to them. Monarchy in particular was falling out of favour.

TIME LINE	40,000BC	10,000	5000	4000	500	AD1	200	4

Above and *below left*:
A French depiction of the events of February 1848.

The precise reasons for the discontent varied from country to country. In some countries nationalism (a thread in the Romantic movement) drove people to demand unification in some cases, or independence in others. In Germany and Italy, the nationalist movement was very strong. Although now these are two united countries, they were then broken up into many separate kingdoms and principalities.

People were also demanding the right to have a say in government, wanting the right to vote in democratic elections. In Britain, the Chartists demanded a range of reforms that included the right of all men to vote. They presented their petition to the British Parliament in 1842, but it was rejected. A big Chartist demonstration was held in London, but the meeting passed off without violence.

There were centres of revolt all over Europe, in London, Paris, Berlin, Frankfurt, Prague, Warsaw, Vienna, Budapest, Milan, Venice and Rome. In France the outbreak of revolution was particularly fierce. Parisian revolutionaries attacked government buildings, overthrew the monarchy, declared a Second Republic, and installed the nephew of Napoleon, Louis Napoleon, as 'Prince-President'.

In Austria, the Emperor Ferdinand abdicated in favour of Franz Josef, and in most countries the ruling elites found ways to hang onto power.

CHRONOLOGY OF EVENTS
1848

2 Feb

Ferdinand II of Naples proclaims a liberal constitution.

24 Feb

King Louis Philippe of France abdicates in favour of his grandson the Comte de Paris, but a Republic is established under Lamartine.

14 Mar

The Pope reluctantly grants a constitution for the Papal States.

17 Mar

Revolution begins in Berlin, capital of Prussia.

26 Mar

Demands for reform in Spain are quickly crushed.

25 Apr

Emperor Ferdinand I of Austria grants a constitution.

7 Sep

Serfdom is abolished in Austria.

2 Dec

Ferdinand I of Austria abdicates in favour of his nephew Franz Josef.

10 Dec

Louis-Napoleon is elected President of France.

27 Dec

The German National Assembly in Frankfurt proclaims the fundamental rights of political and national freedom.

Literature:
Stendhal, Dickens, Tolstoy
AD 1800

The great literary figures of the nineteenth century were like all great figures, as Tolstoy himself saw, creatures of circumstance. Stendhal and Tolstoy were rootless young men who found themselves caught up in the maelstrom of war, which changed and intensified their thinking and gave them great subjects for their novels. Dickens responded passionately to the great social evils of his time, poverty, deprivation, greed and human exploitation.

Stendhal

Stendhal, pen name of Henri Beyle (1783–1842), was born in Grenoble. During his Bohemian youth he wrote plays. He was offered a post in the war ministry and from 1800 followed Napoleon's campaigns across Europe. After the fall of Napoleon he retired to Italy and began to write books. In 1821 the Austrians expelled him from Italy and he returned to France. His great masterpieces were *Le Rouge et le Noir* (1830) and *La Chartreuse de Parme* (1839). Neither of these was widely understood during Stendhal's lifetime, yet they proved to be profoundly influential nineteenth century French novels.

Charles Dickens

Charles Dickens (1812–1870) was born in Portsmouth. His father was made redundant, and then sent to the Marshalsea, a debtors' prison. The young Dickens was sent to a blacking factory at Hungerford Market, where he worked all day sticking

| TIME LINE | 40,000BC | 10,000 | 5000 | 4000 | 500 | AD 1 | 200 | 4 |

labels on bottles. This experience of deprivation and poverty embittered him and drove him to write impassioned novels that focused on the cruelties and social injustices he and other young people had to endure in Victorian England. He was an actor, and his public readings of his novels were hugely popular.

Leo Tolstoy

Leo Tolstoy (1828–1910) led a dissolute life in town before joining an artillery regiment in the Caucasus (1851). His literary career began, rather oddly, with an autobiographical trilogy. When the Crimean War broke out he commanded a battery in the defence of Sebastopol. After his horrific experiences in the war he settled on his Volga estate and spent six years writing *War and Peace* (1869), which some consider the greatest novel ever written. This portrays 'great men' as creatures of circumstance and victory in battle as the outcome of chance. Tolstoy lived like a peasant. His influence was considerable; he corresponded with Gandhi, who adopted his doctrines of the simple life and non-resistance.

CHRONOLOGY OF EVENTS
AD 1822 – 1882

Stendhal

1822 *Armance.*

1830 *Le Rouge et le Noir.*

1839 *La Chartreuse de Parme.*

Dickens

1843 *Martin Chuzzlewit.*

1850 *David Copperfield.*

1853 *Bleak House.*

1861 *Great Expectations.*

1865 *Our Mutual Friend.*

Tolstoy

1869 *War and Peace.*

1876 *Anna Karenina.*

1882 *A Confession.*

Left: Leo Tolstoy, 1828–1910.
Opposite page, top:
Stendhal, 1783–1842.
Opposite page, bottom:
Charles Dickens, 1812–1870.

Music: Beethoven & Wagner
AD 1800

OVERVIEW ❖ OVERVIEW ❖ OVERVIEW ❖ OVERVIEW ❖ OVERVIEW

In the nineteenth century, the language of music developed in an extraordinary way, due to the Romantic movement's emphasis on the exploration of the mind of the individual and the cult of the artist as hero. Beethoven, struggling against his deafness, was a perfect Romantic hero. Wagner, with his musical genius and unscrupulous 'borrowing' of money and wives, was a perfect Romantic anti-hero.

Ludwig van Beethoven

Ludwig van Beethoven (1770–1827) was born in Bonn. His unstable, ambitious father trained him to be another Mozart which, incredibly, did not destroy the boy's love of music. In 1787, at the age of 17, he visited Vienna, played for Mozart and may have had some lessons with him. In 1792, Haydn agreed to teach Beethoven. By 1802 he had composed 3 piano concertos and two symphonies, but was already suffering from depression induced by his increasing deafness. The Third Symphony, the *Eroica*, written in 1803, is a tribute to and an embodiment of the Romantic ideal of the hero. Beethoven's single opera, *Fidelio*, develops the simple themes of fidelity, personal liberation and the symbolic passage from darkness to light.

The great works of his final period, the *Missa Solemnis* and the *Ninth Symphony*, reach up to new heights. They are ambitious, visionary pieces, with the now totally deaf composer himself as hero.

Beethoven bridged the transition from Classical to Romantic with total conviction. Like Goethe, Beethoven was a giant creative force, extending the existing forms of the concerto, symphony and string quartet as well as redefining what music was capable of expressing.

TIME LINE	40,000BC	10,000	5000	4000	500	AD1	200	4

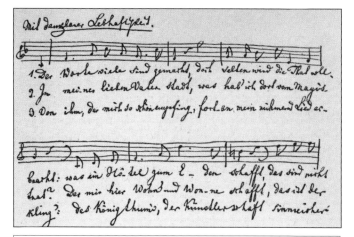

Wagner score for a humorous song, dedicated to Louis Kraft, proprietor of the Hotel Prusse at Leipzig, in gratitude for an enjoyable stay.

Richard Wagner

Richard Wagner (1813–1883) was born in Leipzig. His early compositions were undistinguished, but *The Flying Dutchman* (1843) was a more mature and craftsmanlike piece. Wagner made the mistake of involving himself in politics and his part in the 1848 revolt in Dresden would have resulted in a decade in prison, but for his escape from Saxony. He spent his exile plotting a come-back in Germany, and working on the great *Ring of the Nibelung* project, which was finally performed with King Ludwig II of Bavaria's help in 1876.

Wagner's operas show a remarkable development from imitations of Weber and Meyerbeer to a new 'artwork of the future', a psychological approach to opera in which the music interweaves themes representing several ideas and emotions at once. This use of leitmotivs, or musical archetypes, looks forward to the twentieth century psychoanalytical ideas of Carl Gustav Jung (1875–1961). Wagner represents the fullest flowering of Romanticism in music.

CHRONOLOGY OF EVENTS
AD 1770 – 1883

Beethoven

1770 Born in Bonn.

1795 *Second Piano Concerto.*

1799 *Pathetique Sonata.*

1800 *First Symphony.*

1805 *Third Symphony, Fidelio.*

1808 *Fifth and Sixth Symphonies.*

1810 *Egmont Overture.*

1824 *Missa Solemnis; Ninth Symphony.*

1827 Dies in Vienna.

Wagner

1813 Born in Leipzig.

1843 *The Flying Dutchman.*

1845 *Tannhauser.*

1850 *Lohengrin.*

1865 *Tristan and Isolde.*

1870 *Siegfried Idyll.*

1876 *The Ring of the Nibelung.*

1882 *Parsifal.*

1883 Dies in Venice.

The American Civil War

AD 1861

The southern states of the USA had relied heavily on slaves to work on cotton and other plantations and by 1860 the South quarrelled with the non-slave North especially over what southerners felt was undue federal interference from Washington. The matter was settled by the victory of the North in the Civil War (1861–65) after which the slaves were freed. Bitterness between North and South was felt in the country for many decades afterwards.

US President, Abraham Lincoln . 1860–1865.

Abraham Lincoln and the North

The North of the United States was heavily industrialized and slavery had been abandoned. The South in comparison was still predominantly agricultural, with farms worked by slaves. The southern economy was based on cotton, and planters depended on slave labour. In 1860, Abraham Lincoln became president. He opposed the extension of slavery to western territories. Fearing he would abolish slavery everywhere, southern states split from the Union to form the Confederacy. In April 1861, Confederate troops fired on Union forces in Fort Sumter, South Carolina. Lincoln called volunteers to defend the union. The two sides went to war.

The Talented Southern Commanders

At first, able Confederate generals such as 'Stonewall' Jackson, won victories. The North had more resources,

TIME LINE	40,000BC	10,000	5000	4000	500	AD1	200	40

with larger and better equipped armies, but the South had some of the greatest commanders of the century. Stonewall Jackson, J. E. B. Stuart, Jubal Early and their senior commander, Robert E. Lee, sustained the South far beyond their true capacity. Gradually, however, the South was worn down. Early in April 1865, Robert E. Lee surrendered after the Battle of Northern Virginia had seen the deaths of over 600,000 people.

All Men Are Created Equal

In late 1865, Congress approved Lincoln's proclamation of 1863 that all slaves were to be freed. After the war, ex-slaves were given land to replant, but lacking the resources the conditions they lived in were little better than slavery. Some southerners refused to accept that slaves were no longer slaves, and in 1866 the Ku Klux Klan, a secret society, was founded to reassert white supremacy and the abuse of black people continued through the twentieth century.

Gettysburg. A heroic charge by Confederate General Pickett and his men fails to dislodge the Federal position.

CHRONOLOGY OF EVENTS
AD 1860 – 1865

1860
Abraham Lincoln becomes US president.

12 April 1861
Civil War starts when Confederate troops under General Beauregard fire on Union forces at Fort Sumter.

2 Oct 1861
Battle of Ball's Bluff. Confederate victory.

8 Mar 1862
First naval battle between ironclad ships. The Confederate Merrimac sinks the Cumberland.

30 Aug 1862
Second Battle of Bull Run. Confederates win.

1-3 Jul 1863
Battle of Gettysburg. The North wins the biggest battle of the war.

19 Nov 1863
Gettysburg Address; Lincoln proclaims that all slaves are to be freed.

23–25 Nov 1863
Battle of Chattanooga. Confederates defeated.

3 Apr 1865
General Grant captures Richmond, the capital of the South.

9 April 1865
General Robert E. Lee surrenders to General Ulysses Grant, bringing the Civil War to an end.

14 Apr 1865
Lincoln is assassinated in Washington.

A Revolution in Communications

AD 1885

OVERVIEW ❖ OVERVIEW ❖ OVERVIEW ❖ OVERVIEW ❖ OVERVIEW

Towards the end of the nineteenth century some significant developments were made in communications, both in methods of transport (bicycles, cars, trams and planes) and methods of transmitting information (by post, typewriter, telephone and radio).

Means of transport

The first bicycles were uncomfortable to ride because they had metal tyres. By the end of the nineteenth century significant improvements had been made to the design so that bicycles became much more attractive as a form a transport. The 'penny-farthing', with its two different-sized wheels, was designed in 1883. It had the advantage of tyres made of solid rubber, but the disadvantage of hoisting the rider high off the ground. Manufacturers soon settled on the 'safety bicycle', with two same-sized wheels. The (inflatable) pneumatic tyre made cycling much more comfortable. The motorcycle was invented soon after, with the first one sold in 1894.

The Penny Farthing.

At about the same time the car was being developed, again using first solid rubber tyres, then pneumatic tyres. The first motor cars were hand crafted in Germany in 1885. Trams powered by overhead cables were invented in Berlin in 1881. Mass production of motor cars followed in 1908, with Henry Ford's Model T.

As part of the same remarkable surge in technological development in Europe and North America, the first flights in powered aircraft came in the same decade. The Wright brothers successfully flew their plane in 1903.

Henry Ford's Model T.

TIME LINE	40,000BC	10,000	5000	4000	500	AD1	200	40

Orville Wright, American pioneer aviator, and his biplane.

Communicating messages

Communication of ideas and information took several steps forward with the development of the postage stamp, telephone and radio. Couriers and postal services had been developed in Britain for over a century, but a big step forward was made in 1840, with the introduction of prepaid stamps, paid for by the sender of the letter. Then, in 1875, the telephone was invented by Alexander Graham Bell, which made it possible for people in different cities to hold a conversation, though very few people had telephones in their homes until the 1920s. Radio waves, discovered in 1888 by Heinrich Hertz, were exploited by Marconi in 1901 to send Morse code messages across oceans. The typewriter, invented as early as 1808, was not mass produced until 1873; then it made the communication of information much easier.

An Ericsson Table Phone, 1892. Two generator magnets support the instrument and the induction coil is contained in the pedestal.

CHRONOLOGY OF EVENTS
AD 1840 – 1908

1840

Introduction of pre-paid postage stamps.

1873

The typewriter is mass produced.

1875

The telephone is invented by Alexander Graham Bell.

1881

Trams powered by overhead cables are invented in Berlin.

1883

The 'penny-farthing' is designed.

1884

The ladies' bicycle, with no cross-bar, is invented.

1885

The 'safety bicycle' is invented by John Starley. The first motor cars are hand crafted by Karl Benz. The first motorbicycle prototypes are made by Daimler and Maybach.

1901

Radio is developed by Marconi to send Morse code messages.

1903

The Wright brothers successfully fly their plane.

1908

Mass production of motor cars begins.

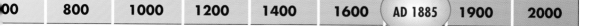

The Scramble for Africa: Imperialism & African Plight

AD 1850

OVERVIEW ❖ OVERVIEW ❖ OVERVIEW ❖ OVERVIEW ❖ OVERVIEW

Missionaries, explorers and traders inadvertently established areas of European influence, which gradually gained momentum. By the end of the century seven European powers were competing to own as much of Africa as possible, redrawing the map with little or no regard for the Africans who lived there.

Europeans knew little and understood nothing about Africa, believing that forcing Christianity and cash crops on the Native Africans would do them good. The travels of missionaries like Mary Kingsley and David Livingstone did much to excite European interest in Africa. British and North American explorers such as Burton, Speke and Stanley traced the courses of major rivers, largely for the sake of correcting the maps.

Gradually, European countries developed control over specific areas. By 1850, the Portuguese, French, Dutch and British had established 'bridgeheads' on the coasts. The big Muslim empires of the interior, Elhajiomar and Sokoto, remained independent for the time

At Mangoche, Nyasaland, Yao tribespersons attend a 'hearers' instruction class in Christian teaching.

TIME LINE	40,000BC	10,000	5000	4000	500	AD1	200

being, but the disruption of African society by over 200 years of the slave trade was well advanced.

Rivalry broke out among the European powers to grab colonies in what became known as 'the scramble for Africa'. Germany, Spain, Italy and Belgium joined France, Portugal and Britain in an empire-building race for territory. Conflicts quickly flared up between France and Britain over rival claims in West Africa and Egypt. In 1884, the heads of the European states involved attended a conference in Berlin to draw lines on the map of Africa, staking their claims.

The Africans themselves had no say in any of this and their economic and cultural needs were rarely considered. The Native Africans were treated with as little concern as the Native North Americans. The Europeans agreed frontiers that disregarded tribal areas and the resources the native people depended upon. The European colonists who migrated to Africa took the most productive farm land and generally treated the Africans as inferiors. The effects of imperialism on Africa were destructive and long-lasting, though profitable for the white settlers.

CHRONOLOGY OF EVENTS
AD 1849 – 1895

1849
Livingstone becomes first European to cross the Kalahari Desert.

1855
Livingstone discovers the Victoria Falls.

1856
Livingstone completes his crossing of Africa, reaching the Mozambique coast.

1857
Speke discovers Lake Victoria and infers that it is the source of the Nile.

1860
Speke tracks the White Nile as it flows out of Lake Victoria.

1867
Diamonds are discovered in the Vaal valley, South Africa.

1868
Livingstone discovers Lakes Mweru and Bangweulu.

1880
Each year, from now until 1914, another quarter of a million square miles of African territory falls under colonial control.

1884
Berlin conference to settle colonial claims to African territories.

1893
Mary Kingsley's first journey through West Africa.

1895
Mary Kingsley's second journey through West Africa.

The British Empire

AD 1850

OVERVIEW ❖ OVERVIEW ❖ OVERVIEW ❖ OVERVIEW ❖ OVERVIEW

Britain acquired huge territories in the contest among European powers to acquire colonies. There were early signs that the native peoples did not want to be governed by the British, but they were ignored. The British Empire was a huge trading operation, with Britain siphoning cheap raw materials from the colonies and in turn using the Empire as a captive market for manufactured goods.

By 1850, the 200 million people living in the subcontinent of India were ruled by a private company, the British East India Company. It had lost its trade monopoly and made its way by taxation, just like a state government. The Indian rebellion against the Company's rule and general discontent at British interference in the Indian way of life in 1857 came as a great surprise to the British who, characteristically, could see nothing wrong with their imperialist strategy.

When the revolt ended in 1858, control of India passed formally to the British government. The seeds of Indian nationalism were sown, and the drive towards independence gained momentum, not only in India but throughout the Empire, during the first half of the twentieth century.

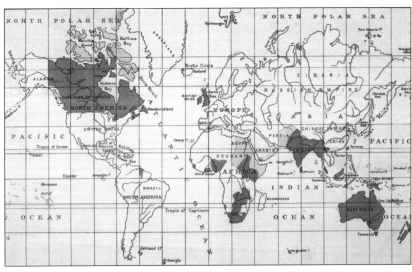

Map showing the extent of the British Empire circa 1880.

TIME LINE	40,000BC	10,000	5000	4000	500	AD1	200	40

British possessions in Africa included the Gold Coast (Ghana), Nigeria, and a string of huge territories from South Africa to Egypt. It was Cecil Rhodes's ambition to make Africa British 'from Cape to Cairo'. Australia and Canada were two more huge possessions; although Canada was granted home rule in 1867 and Australia independence in 1901, both remained in the Empire. By the end of the Victorian era, the British Empire was a global enterprise, embracing a quarter of the land and people in the world. There was great pride in the Empire. Every schoolroom had a world map showing the British Empire coloured red; the Mercator projection made Canada seem even bigger.

Lord Frederick Sleigh Roberts, British soldier who served in India, Afghanistan and South Africa.

The Empire was a huge commercial and administrative operation, the colonies supplying cheap raw materials and functioning as captive markets for goods manufactured in Britain. The Empire also created many jobs for administrators and servicemen. There was a missionary aspect to it as well; the British persuaded themselves that they were helping the colonies to develop. Meanwhile, Britain grew rich off its Empire.

CHRONOLOGY OF EVENTS
AD 1850 – 1901

1850

The Indian subcontinent is still governed by the British East India Company.

1857

The Indian rebellion against the Company's rule begins.

1858

The Indian revolt ends. Control of India passes to the British government.

1867

Canada is granted home rule, remaining in the Empire.

1875

Britain gains control of the Suez Canal, shortening the sea route to India by 8,050 km.

1884

Cecil Rhodes acquires Bechuanaland (Botswana) as a protectorate.

1889

Rhodes acquires the charter for the British South Africa Company (whose territories later become Zambia and Zimbabwe).

1890

Rhodes becomes prime minister of Cape Colony.

1901

Australia is granted independence, remaining in the Empire.

Science & Medicine

AD 1800

The discovery of invisible germs and bacteria led the way to programmes of pasteurization and immunization, which saved countless lives. Charles Darwin, Louis Agassiz and Sigmund Freud put forward revolutionary new models of reality to explain the worlds around us and within us.

Medicine

A great breakthrough in medicine was the discovery of germs and bacteria as causes of infection and disease by Louis Pasteur (1822–1895) in the 1840s and Robert Koch (1840–1910) in the 1880s. More than 20 diseases became preventable by immunization. Pasteur's discoveries led to pasteurization, the treatment of food to prevent it from being infected by bacteria.

Another major advance in the 1840s was the introduction of ether as an anaesthetic, first for dental work, then for surgery; this rendered surgery painless and reduced the likelihood of patients dying of shock while undergoing major surgery. In 1865, antiseptics were introduced, which greatly increased the chances of full recovery after surgery; previously many had died of infection.

A new invention was the hypodermic needle. Precision engineering now made the manufacture of instruments like this possible. Even more radical was the discovery of x-rays by Wilhelm Rontgen in 1895; this made it possible see inside the body and make more accurate diagnoses.

The Hypodermic Needle was invented in 1853, and X-rays were invented in 1895.

| **TIME LINE** | 40,000BC | 10,000 | 5000 | 4000 | 500 | AD1 | 200 | 40 |

Science

A great advance in theoretical science came with the publication of *The Origin of Species* by Charles Darwin (1809–1882). The theory of natural selection offered an explanation of the way animals had evolved since the beginning of life. It was an alternative to the biblical model of the 'seven days of Creation', which increasing numbers of educated people found difficult to reconcile with the results of scientific enquiry. The direct challenge even so created a storm of controversy when Darwin's book was published.

At the same time, the naturalist and glaciologist Louis Agassiz (1807–1873) put forward, in *Systeme glaciaire* (1847), his equally revolutionary idea that there had been an Ice Age when large areas of Europe were covered with glaciers.

At the end of the century, Sigmund Freud (1856–1939) invented the new science of psychoanalysis. He explored illnesses that had no physical cause, and came to the conclusion that they originated in an unconscious part of the mind.

Charles Darwin's theory of evolution directly contradicted the story of creation as recorded in the Holy Bible.

CHRONOLOGY OF EVENTS
AD 1833 – 1900
1833
Charles Lyell: *Principles of Geology.*
1847
Louis Agassiz: *The Glacial System.*
1859
Charles Darwin: *The Origin of Species.*
1863
Charles Lyell: *The Antiquity of Man.*
1864
Louis Pasteur pioneers the airborne germ theory of infection.
1865
Joseph Lister pioneers the use of antiseptics on wound dressings.
1880
Pasteur develops a chicken cholera vaccine.
1882
Robert Koch pioneers bacteriology, isolating the tuberculosis bacillus.
1885
Pasteur develops a rabies vaccine.
1888
The Pasteur Institute is founded.
1895
Wilhelm Rontgen discovers x-rays.
1896
Koch discovers a cure for rinderpest.
1900
Sigmund Freud: *The Interpretation of Dreams.*

THE
TWENTIETH
CENTURY

The Arms Race

AD 1900

Imperialism and the contest to acquire colonies brought several nations into conflict around the turn of the twentieth century, leading to an arms race. Armies were enlarged and fleets were modernized, as nations prepared themselves for large-scale conflict.

The contest to collect colonial possessions all round the world sharpened the long-standing rivalry among the great imperialist powers. The colonized world now absorbed 560 million people. Limited conflicts broke out: between USA and Spain (1898), between Britain and France at Fashoda (1898), between Britain and the Boers in South Africa (1899–1902), between Germany and France over Morocco (1911). It would not be long before open war broke out on a larger scale among several countries.

A big armaments industry developed in Europe, with many advances in weaponry. New machine guns were invented that could repeat fire more rapidly than before. As the arms race accelerated and war seemed more likely, national armies were expanded and fleets of powerful new battleships, called 'dreadnoughts', were launched. The two sides raced to make deadly new weapons, such as poison gas.

The Dreadnought was the most advanced battleship on the sea, a model to be copied for years to follow.

TIME LINE	40,000BC	10,000	5000	4000	500	AD1	200

One particular European trouble-spot was the Balkans (Yugoslavia). Serbia had been successful in the Balkan Wars and its new-found power posed a threat to the Austro-Hungarian Empire. Austria-Hungary feared that Serbia would expand and create a rival Slav Empire; there were many Slavs living in Austria-Hungary. Russia, as a Slav nation, would be likely to take Serbia's side. Another problem was the newly-unified Prussian-led Germany, which had also become very powerful and was a threat to its neighbours. The Germans were determined to enter, somewhat belatedly, the race to collect African colonies, and a dispute arose with France over Morocco. Britain too was threatened by German aspirations on the high seas, where Britain assumed supremacy. Russia meanwhile was anxious about German aspirations in the east, as there was a danger that Russia's access to the Mediterranean via the Black Sea would be cut off.

These various national interests led to the European states forming two rival groups. France and Britain formed an Entente Cordiale in 1904; Russia joined in 1907 to form a Triple Entente. In between, Italy, Germany and Austria-Hungary formed a Triple Alliance. The polarization into two large power blocs meant that almost any conflict would inevitably draw other countries in, one by one.

CHRONOLOGY OF EVENTS
AD 1895 – 1913

1895

The Kiel Canal is opened, allowing German ships to pass unsupervised between the Baltic and the North Sea.

1898

Spanish-American War.

1898

Fashoda: diplomatic incident between Britain and France over claims to Egypt.

1899

Boer War begins. President Kruger of the Boer Republic tries to stop the British acquiring the Transvaal gold mines.

1902

Boer War ends. Britain acquires South Africa. Germany, Austria and Italy renew the 1882 Triple Alliance.

1904

France and Britain form an Entente Cordiale.

1906

The Dreadnought, first of a new generation of battleships carrying ten 12-inch guns, is launched in Britain.

1907

Russia joins the Entente Cordiale to form a Triple Entente. The Triple Alliance is renewed.

1913

The First Balkan War is resolved. The Second Balkan War breaks out immediately.

The First World War (1)

AD 1914

OVERVIEW ❖ OVERVIEW ❖ OVERVIEW ❖ OVERVIEW ❖ OVERVIEW

The networks of alliances meant that just one incident, the assassination of the Austro-Hungarian Crown Prince, led to continent-wide war (1914–1918). It was fought mainly on land, and on two fronts, the Western Front and the Eastern Front. There was only one major sea-battle, Jutland. Germany's u-boat blockade was a miscalculation which brought America into the war.

Archduke Franz Ferdinand.

The start of the First World War

When Archduke Franz Ferdinand, heir to the Austro-Hungarian empire, was assassinated at Sarajevo in Serbia (28 June 1914), Austria declared war on Serbia (28 July). The Russian army was mobilized to defend Serbia. The Triple Alliance obliged Germany, Austria-Hungary's ally, to declare war on Russia (1 August) and France, Russia's ally (3 August). To reach France, the German army marched across Belgium, and this invasion of a neutral country made Britain declare war on Germany (4 August).

Battles

On the Western Front (France's north-east frontier) many bloody battles were fought, such as Passchendaele, Verdun, the Marne, Ypres and the Somme. Millions of men lost their lives. The Allies (French, British, Australian, Canadian, New Zealand and South African troops) fought from networks of squalid trenches across a strip of ground called No Man's Land.

The Eastern Front (Baltic to Black Sea) was also lined by trenches, where the Russians retreated after being defeated by the Germans in September 1914. In a badly miscalculated plan, British, Australian and New Zealand troops were sent in

TIME LINE	40,000BC	10,000	5000	4000	500	AD1	200

1915 to reinforce the Russian effort in the east, where they tried to take the Dardanelles, the access route to the Black Sea; they were overwhelmed by a powerful and determined Turkish force and the Allies suffered huge losses.

War at sea

There was only one great sea battle in the First World War, the Battle of Jutland in 1916. The outcome was inconclusive, with more British than German warships lost, but the German fleet was confined to port for the rest of the war and British supremacy unchallenged.

France and Britain relied on Canadian and American supplies of food and weapons. The Germans used submarines (u-boats) to sink the supply ships as they tried to cross the Atlantic. From 1917 they attacked any ship in the waters round Britain. The Germans knew this would provoke America into joining in the war, but hoped Britain and France would surrender first. This did not succeed because a convoy system was adopted, the unarmed merchant ships sailing in groups shepherded by naval vessels.

Wounded soldiers return from the Battle of the Somme, July 1916.

CHRONOLOGY OF EVENTS
AD 1914 – 1916

28 Jul 1914

Archduke Franz Ferdinand is assassinated at Sarajevo in Serbia. Austria declares war on Serbia.

1 Aug

Germany declares war on Russia.

3 Aug

Germany declares war on France, invading Belgium.

4 Aug

Britain declares war on Germany.

5–12 Sep

Battle of the Marne.

30 Oct–24 Nov

Battle of Ypres.

2 Dec

Battle of Cracow.

25 Apr 1915

British, Australian and New Zealand troops land on the Gallipoli Peninsula but are pinned down by Turkish artillery.

Jan 1916

British troops withdraw from Gallipoli after suffering huge losses.

21 Feb–11 Jul 1916

Battle of Verdun.

31 May–1 Jun

Battle of Jutland.

1 Jul–13 Nov 1916

Battle of the Somme. The biggest and bloodiest engagement on the Western Front: 420,000 British troops are killed.

The First World War (2)

AD 1918

The withdrawal of Russia from the war released huge numbers of German troops for service on the Western Front. There they were met by newly arrived American troops. The two sides were evenly matched, but Germany was starving and forced to surrender in 1918. The Versailles Peace Settlement demanded huge sums of money from Germany in compensation and took away its colonies.

The Western Front

The arrival of American troops on the Western Front in 1917 meant that the Allies could launch fresh attacks on the Germans. In 1918 Russia dropped out of the war, so German troops could be diverted from the Eastern to the Western Front. There were now over 3.5 million German soldiers on the Western Front, and in March they were able to push through towards Paris. In August British tanks (which first appeared at the Somme in September 1916) broke the German line at Amiens and the Germans retreated. Behind the Western Front, the German people were nearing starvation thanks to a naval blockade, and ready to surrender.

The end of the war and its aftermath

On 11 November Germany surrendered, the German Kaiser abdicated and the fighting stopped. 10 million soldiers had died, 20 million had been wounded. The loss of so many young men was a tragedy, but it also meant that after the war many women gained more freedom and more equality.

The Versailles Peace Settlement (1919–23) was designed to punish Germany. Germany would lose

British and US soldiers celebrate the Allied victory in Germany.

TIME LINE	**40,000BC**	**10,000**	**5000**	**4000**	**500**	**AD1**	**200**	4

Jubilant peace celebrations in Piccadilly Circus, London, at the end of the Great War.

some of its homeland and colonies, and pay huge sums of money in compensation to the Allies. The German economy collapsed, with the value of money falling very fast (hyperinflation).

The League of Nations

The Versailles Peace Settlement also set up the League of Nations to maintain world peace. It would settle disputes by discussion, not by fighting. Rivalry among the members weakened the League of Nations so much that few people took any notice of it by the 1930s. It was replaced, after the Second World War, by the United Nations.

The League set up mandates (agreements to give one country control over another), in effect sharing out the German colonies among the Allies. Britain became responsible for Iraq (1920–1932), Palestine (1922–1948), Tanganyika (Tanzania) (until independence in 1961). South Africa became responsible for German South-West Africa (Namibia). France became responsible for Syria (1920–1946). These mandates were to create fresh rounds of colonial problems.

CHRONOLOGY OF EVENTS
AD 1917 – 1920

17 Jan 1917

Germans announce the beginning of 'unrestricted submarine warfare' aimed at supply ships crossing the Atlantic.

Mar 1917

The Germans push through towards Paris.

6 Apr 1917

USA declares war on Germany.

9 Apr 1917

Battle of Arras. Canadian troops take Vimy Ridge.

31 July–10 Nov 1917

Battle of Passchendaele. 400,000 British soldiers are killed.

Aug 1918

Battle of Amiens. British tanks break the German line and the Germans retreat.

8 Nov 1918

The German Kaiser abdicates.

11 Nov 1918

Germany surrenders. Fighting ceases.

18 Jan 1919

The Versailles Peace Conference opens. Huge sums of money are exacted from Germany in compensation.

25 Jan 1919

The Peace Conference votes to create a League of Nations.

15 Nov 1920

The League of Nations meets for the first time.

The Russian Revolution

AD 1917

OVERVIEW ❖ OVERVIEW ❖ OVERVIEW ❖ OVERVIEW ❖ OVERVIEW

Reforms in the late nineteenth century came too late to avert a revolution in Russia. The 1905 revolution was crushed and revolutionary leaders left Russia, biding their time. The First World War distracted the Russian government and weakened the economy. The March 1917 revolution overthrew the monarchy, but the moderate Kerensky government was in its turn overthrown in the 'October' 1917 revolution when Lenin returned from exile to set up a communist regime. A civil war between communist Reds and moderate Whites was won by the communists in 1921.

After the Crimean War, Tsar Alexander II realised his mainly agricultural country needed modernization. One major reform was the freeing of serfs, tied farm workers who had few rights. Another was the democratization of government. But radicals were dissatisfied and riots and strikes broke out. In 1881 Alexander II was assassinated, and the new tsar, Alexander III, reversed all his predecessor's reforms. Books and newspapers were censored

Lenin 1870–1924.

and police were given new powers. Striking workers were fired on by troops in 1905. Then a new tsar, Nicholas II, promised civil rights and a Duma (parliament), but his promises were not kept and elections were rigged to keep reformers out of the Duma. Government opponents were arrested and the leading revolutionaries fled the country.

In the Second World War, the Russian economy began to collapse. Many Russians starved. Riots broke out in Petrograd (St Petersburg) in March 1917. Troops ordered to disperse the crowds joined the rioters, the Tsar abdicated and a temporary government was set up under Prince Lvov, who was quickly succeeded by Alexander Kerensky as chief minister. The Russian Revolution was not over, though. The Bolshevik leader, Lenin, returned to Petrograd to turn

TIME LINE	40,000BC	10,000	5000	4000	500	AD1	200	4

Russia into a communist state. The Bolsheviks seized power in November 1917 (called the 'October' revolution because Russia used a different calendar). Lenin's new government made peace with Germany, moved the capital to Moscow, and began breaking up the big country estates to give land to the peasants. Church property was taken. Banks were nationalized.

White Russians (anti-communists) opposed these moves and civil war broke out. The Whites were finally defeated by the (Bolshevik) Red Army in 1921. The state was renamed the Union of Soviet Socialist Republics (USSR).

By the end of the Revolution, 100,000 people had been killed, including the royal family, and 2 million had left Russia. Lenin remained leader until he died in 1924, when a power struggle broke out between Leon Trotsky (1879–1940) and Josef Stalin (1879–1953). The ruthless Stalin won and became a vicious dictator, controlling the USSR until his own death in 1953, having ordered the exiled Trotsky's assassination in Mexico in 1940.

St Basil's Cathedral. Red Square, Moscow.

CHRONOLOGY OF EVENTS
AD 1905 – 1921

9 Jan 1905
Revolution breaks out in St Petersburg.

17 Oct 1905
The Potemkin mutiny at Odessa.

9 Dec 1905
Revolution suppressed by the tsar.

24 May 1906
Tsar Nicholas II grants universal suffrage.

1 Sep 1911
Prime minister Stolypin is assassinated.

15 Mar 1917
The Tsar abdicates. Riots erupt in Petrograd.

16 Mar 1917
Grand Duke Michael abdicates, in favour of a provisional government.

Apr 1917
Lenin returns from exile.

6 Nov 1917
'October Revolution'. Troops storm the Winter Palace in Petrograd at Lenin's orders.

7 Nov 1917
The Kerensky government falls. Lenin forms a government. Civil war between communist Reds and moderate Whites breaks out.

16 Jul 1918
The Tsar and his family are shot (by Reds).

14 Nov 1920
Civil war ends as the White Army evacuates to Constantinople.

1921
The communist state is renamed the Union of Soviet Socialist Republics (USSR).

Architecture

AD 1900

OVERVIEW ❖ OVERVIEW ❖ OVERVIEW ❖ OVERVIEW ❖ OVERVIEW

The use of reinforced concrete and steel made new shapes possible. Art Nouveau was still popular. The new clean lines of the International style and the Bauhaus school produced a distinctive twentieth century look, as did the skyscrapers of Frank Lloyd Wright and Mies van der Rohe.

Many advanced new buildings used steel and reinforced concrete, which made possible entirely new shapes. The 'International' style which emerged in the first half of the twentieth century used large areas of glass, which became possible with steel structures. Plain lines and rectangles were common features, the plainness emphasized by white paint. A classic early example of this style was designed by the great French architect Le Corbusier (Charles Jeanneret, 1887–1965). It is the Villa Savoye at Poissy in France, a building on the pilotis (stilts) which are almost a Le Corbusier signature, with windows arranged in long strips, and a flat roof that doubles as a garden. The Bauhaus school of architecture, founded in 1919 by Walter Gropius (1883–1969) was a branch of this International style.

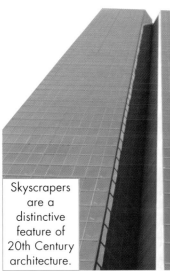

Skyscrapers are a distinctive feature of 20th Century architecture.

Space was in great demand in city centres, and this led to the construction of taller and taller buildings. One great pioneer of the new skyscraper style was Mies van der Rohe. He designed blocks with metal frames and thin walls of glass and metal. Another great pioneer of the skyscraper was Frank Lloyd Wright (1867–1959). Wright also designed some revolutionary small buildings too, such as his own house, Taliesin (1911), in Wisconsin and another, called Falling Water, near Pittsburgh.

Side by side with the International style was the Art Nouveau style. This was really a reference back to the last decade of the

TIME LINE	40,000BC	10,000	5000	4000	500	AD1	200	4C

nineteenth century, but the use of concrete made flowing organic lines developed from natural forms possible.

Art Deco was a richly decorative 1920s and 1930s style, with lots of detail, but using geometric shapes. The most spectacular example is the Chrysler Building in New York.

Some major projects seem to have a retro-style of their own. The Hoover Dam, built on the Colorado in 1936, is a simple concrete structure that looks back to a kind of minimalist Art Nouveau style. The Sydney Harbour Bridge built in 1932 could have been designed by Telford or Brunel.

The Chrysler Building, New York, built in the Art Deco style.

CHRONOLOGY OF EVENTS
AD 1900 – 1943

1900

C. H. Townsend: Horniman Museum, London.

1909

Napoleon LeBrun: Metropolitan Life Insurance Tower, New York. 42 storeys, the world's tallest building, until 1913.

1913

Cass Gilbert: Woolworth Building, New York. 60 storeys, the world's tallest building until 1931.

1919

The Bauhaus school of architecture founded by Walter Gropius.

1930

William Van Allen: Chrysler Building in New York. Tallest brick building in the world.

1931

Lamb and Harmon: Empire State Building, New York.

1932

Sydney Harbour Bridge.

1936

Hoover Dam, on the Colorado.

1936

Joseph Strauss: Golden Gate Bridge, San Francisco.

1943

The Pentagon, Virginia.

Communications

AD 1900

OVERVIEW ❖ OVERVIEW ❖ OVERVIEW ❖ OVERVIEW ❖ OVERVIEW

Transport was revolutionized by the mass production of cars. The rich still travelled slowly, on luxurious passenger liners which grew larger. The airship was less successful and fell into disfavour after some spectacular disasters. Halfway through the century, the idea of the package holiday with flights was born. Radio, cinema and then television brought new forms of mass entertainment.

Cars were still rich men's toys at the beginning of the century, but mass production brought cars within the financial reach of increasing numbers of people. In 1937, Ferdinand Porsche designed the Volkswagen, the German People's Car. Motor cycles were developed, for people who could not afford cars. Many continued to rely on trains, trams and buses.

Ships became bigger and bigger, as the use of steel for hulls became universal. The Titanic, which sank after scraping against an iceberg in 1912, was 269m long. By the 1930s, ocean liners like the Queen Elizabeth and Queen Mary were over 300m long. These luxurious floating hotels crossed the Atlantic in four days, and were much loved by the rich leisured classes who had time to spend on travel.

Airships (invented in 1902) also travelled slowly, but through the air. They turned out to be dangerously accident-prone and after some high-profile disasters, like the loss of the

The Queen Elizabeth, launched in 1938.

TIME LINE	40,000BC	10,000	5000	4000	500	AD1	200	40

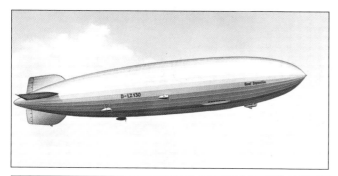

The Zeppelin airship, invented and launched by Count Ferdinand von Zeppelin in 1900.

Hindenburg in 1937, the experiment with this mode of transport came to a close. Planes meanwhile caught on in a big way, playing a minor role in the First World War and a major role in the Second. After the Second World War, when Fascist Spain was economically ostracized by the rest of Europe, the cheap package tour including air flights was invented. Pensioned-off planes and ex-service pilots offered the possibility of cheap air travel to the Mediterranean, beginning a new holiday industry that would boom for 50 years.

In the cities, there were still music halls, where variety shows entertained people. Radio gradually replaced the halls as the great new medium of family entertainment, and people in both cities and remote rural areas had access to it. The cinema was another major new form of entertainment, and a medium for spreading news. Television was invented in 1926 by John Logie Baird, but it would be over 20 years before the technology and the broadcasting system to justify purchasing it was in use in North America and Europe.

CHRONOLOGY OF EVENTS
AD 1902 – 1955

1902

Airships invented.

1919

Radio Corporation of America takes over the Marconi Company.

1922

The British Broadcasting Company is set up.
The Austin Seven, a cheap family car, goes on the market.
The number of telephone subscribers in Britain exceeds one million.

1926

Television is invented by John Logie Baird.

1930

The *R101* airship crashes near Beauvais killing 44.

1934

Luxury passenger liner *Queen Mary* is launched.

1937

Loss of the airship *Hindenburg* killing 36.
Ferdinand Porsche designs the Volkswagen.

1938

Luxury passenger liner *Queen Elizabeth* is launched.

1947

Cheap package tours including air flights start.

1955

First colour television broadcast.

The Rise of Fascism

AD 1920

OVERVIEW ❖ OVERVIEW ❖ OVERVIEW ❖ OVERVIEW ❖ OVERVIEW

During the Great Depression of the 1930s, the simple political solutions offered by fascism held a great attraction in many countries. Italy and Germany had the most flamboyant and conspicuous dictators, Mussolini and Hitler, but other countries had their dictators too. They fed on discontent, national pride, love of military conquest, primitive prejudices, racial hatred and usually involved the persecution of minority groups.

During the 1930s, several countries fell under fascist regimes. Fascism often fed upon racial prejudice, the identification of groups who could be victimized and persecuted as scapegoats for the country's ills. It was also an aggressively patriotic military movement that fed upon a personality cult surrounding the leader – always a dictator. Prominent among these dictators were Benito Mussolini (1883–1945), the Italian dictator, and Adolf Hitler (1889–1945), the German dictator. Ordinary people supported these fascist regimes because they seemed to offer a way out of economic difficulty; this was the time of the Great Depression.

The Fascists came to power in Italy in 1922, with Mussolini as prime minister. He became dictator in 1925, after which he became known as 'The Leader', Il Duce. He cleverly won the support of the Roman Catholic Church by making the Vatican City an independent state in 1929. Mussolini tried belatedly to create an empire in Africa, and invaded Ethiopia in 1935, occupying it until 1941. His followers were officially called Fasci de Combatimento, but they were known informally as 'Blackshirts'.

Hitler brought a very similar political group, the Nationalist Socialist Party, to power in Germany in 1933, having narrowly escaped death when the police machine-gunned a Nazi march in Munich in 1923. Goering was badly wounded and 16 storm troopers were killed. Hitler's great appeal to the German people was that he promised to re-establish Germany as a great nation after its crushing defeat and humiliation at the end of the First World War.

In 1923 in Spain, Primo de Rivera (1878–1930) set up a similar movement, the Falangist

| **TIME LINE** | 40,000BC | 10,000 | 5000 | 4000 | 500 | AD1 | 200 | 4(|

Party. A bitter Civil War broke out between the Falangists and the Republicans (1936–1939), which drew in supporters (for both sides) from other countries, including Britain.

Fascist regimes were favoured in other countries too, such as Portugal. There was even some support in Britain for Oswald Mosley's British Union of Fascists.

1922

The Fascists come to power in Italy with Benito Mussolini as prime minister.

1923

Adolf Hitler and Hermann Goering narrowly escape death when the police machine-gun a Nazi march in Munich.

1925

Mussolini becomes dictator.

1929

Mussolini makes the Vatican City an independent state.

1933

Hitler brings the Nationalist Socialist Party to power in Germany.

1935

Mussolini's troops invade Ethiopia.

1939

The Second World War begins: the Axis (Germany and Italy) and Japan against the Allies (UK, France and USA).

1945

The Second World War ends with defeat for the Axis. Mussolini is shot. Hitler commits suicide.

The Long March: Chiang Kai-Shek & Chairman Mao
AD 1925

OVERVIEW ❖ OVERVIEW ❖ OVERVIEW ❖ OVERVIEW ❖ OVERVIEW

The imperial regime in China was overthrown in 1911, and a Nationalist republic was set up with Sun Yat-sen as president. His successor, Chiang Kai-shek, fought a civil war with the Chinese Communists, led by Mao Zedong, who eventually set up the People's Republic of China in 1949.

Sun Yat-sen and the Nationalists

Educated Chinese had been plotting to overthrow the imperial Chinese regime since the beginning of the twentieth century. In 1905, Sun Yat-sen (1866–1925) founded the Chinese Nationalist Party. Rebellions and plots by the Nationalists and other groups undermined the Manchu government. Yuan Shikai, an influential general, gave his support to a nationalist rebellion in 1911. The Manchu government collapsed and a republic was declared, with Sun Yat-sen as president. When he died in 1925, Chiang Kai-shek (1887–1975) succeeded as leader of both China and the Nationalist Party.

The image of Sun Yat-sen (1866–1925), displayed on the city gate of Taipei in Taiwan.

The Chinese Civil War

To begin with, the Chinese Communist Party helped Chiang Kai-shek, but in 1927 a Civil War broke out between Communists and Nationalists. By 1931, the Communists had set up a rival government, called the Jianxi Soviet, in southern China. Chiang Kai-shek launched several major attacks on them with the intention of wiping them off the face of the Earth. The Communists resisted for a year, before leaving Jiangxi on the Long March.

| TIME LINE | 40,000BC | 10,000 | 5000 | 4000 | 500 | AD1 | 200 | 4(|

Mao Zedong (1893–1976) was chairman of Jiangxi Soviet, and it was he who led the Long March westwards, then north until it reached Yan'an in northern China in October 1935. Only 20,000 of the original 100,000 marchers reached Yan'an, but the Long March (11,265 km long) became a legend, establishing Mao as the Chinese Communist Party leader.

The People's Republic and the Thoughts of Chairman Mao

In 1937, the Japanese invaded China and the Chinese Republic collapsed. In 1949, Mao proclaimed the People's Republic of China, establishing China as a communist state. In the same year, Chiang Kai-shek and his followers fled to Taiwan, where he re-established the Republic of China on a much smaller scale. The civil war had left China poor. Many were starving. Over the next 25 years, Mao worked to transform the country. Collective farms provided the basis of a subsistence economy; 'barefoot doctors' provided medical care for people in rural areas. The Thoughts of Chairman Mao, a little red book, became China's bible.

But in the Cultural Revolution of the 1960s, when he felt threatened by criticism, Mao became cruel and intolerant. Academics were tortured, opponents were executed, and millions died of starvation.

Chiang Kai-shek died in 1975; Mao Zedong died the following year.

Statue of Chairman Mao.

CHRONOLOGY OF EVENTS
AD 1905 – 1976

1905
Sun Yat-sen founds the Chinese Nationalist Party.

1911
The imperial regime in China is overthrown. A Nationalist republic is set up with Sun Yat-sen as president.

1925
Sun Yat-sen dies. He is succeeded by Chiang Kai-shek as leader of both China and the Nationalist Party.

1927
Civil War breaks out between Nationalists and Communists, led by Mao Zedong.

1931
The Communists set up a rival government, the Jianxi Soviet, in southern China.

1935
The Long March.

1937
Japan invades China and the Chinese Republic collapses.

1949
Mao Zedong sets up the People's Republic of China. Chiang Kai-shek and his followers flee to Taiwan.

1975
Chiang Kai-shek dies.

1976
Mao Zedong dies.

The Great Depression & the Onset of Globalization

AD 1929

OVERVIEW ❖ OVERVIEW ❖ OVERVIEW ❖ OVERVIEW ❖ OVERVIEW

Excessive speculation on the American stock market led to a sudden slump in share prices as everyone wanted to sell at once. This was the Wall Street Crash. Many investors lost everything. There was no money for investment in business, so many businesses failed and many people lost their jobs. The Great Depression spread to Europe too; there was high unemployment in USA, Germany and UK. This hugely negative effect of globalization made many seek refuge in nationalism, especially in Germany, leading the way to the Second World War.

The Wall Street Crash

Reckless speculation on the American stock market in the 1920s sent share prices way above their real values. Suddenly, in October 1929, people started selling their shares. Investors wanted to be sure of getting the highest price for their shares, so they sold more and more and the share prices dropped rapidly. On one day 13 million shares were sold on the New York Stock Exchange on Wall Street. Share prices dropped so steeply that many lost all their money. This became known as the Wall Street Crash.

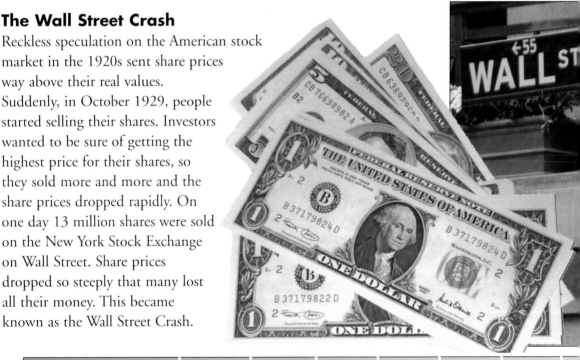

TIME LINE	40,000BC	10,000	5000	4000	500	AD1	200	4

The Great Depression

Banks and businesses closed, because there was no money to invest in business and people had less money to buy goods. Unemployment grew rapidly. By 1932, 12 million people in the USA were unemployed. The American economy was in a serious depression. The situation was worsened by disaster in the Midwest. Drought in the Prairies turned the soil to dust and much of it blew away in the wind. Some farms were stripped of soil; others were buried under drifts of wind-blown dust. Many farmers and farm workers left to try to find work in California.

International repercussions

A system of international loans existed to handle the war reparations that were still being paid by Germany. The Wall Street Crash caused this system to collapse. The effects were not just restricted to America and Europe. European colonies were badly affected, because much of their trade depended on selling raw materials and food to America and Europe; because these markets collapsed, many people involved in production in the colonies also lost their jobs.

This was one of the early signs of the ill effects of globalization. As unrest increased, so nationalism grew, especially in Germany, where there were 6 million people out of work in 1933. This paved the way for the Second World War.

The British economy slumped. In 1935, 200 men marched from Jarrow in the north of England to London, to draw attention to unemployment in the North-East.

CHRONOLOGY OF EVENTS
AD 1929 – 1935

24 Oct 1929

Black Thursday:
The Wall Street Crash begins.

29 Oct 1929

Black Tuesday:
The Dow Jones Industrial Average falls 30 points in one day.

Nov 1929

American loans to Europe cease.

1932

The US economy is in a serious depression. 12 million people in the USA are unemployed. Chancellor Bruning declares that Germany cannot and will not resume reparations payments.

1933

6 million people are out of work in Germany. Nationalism grows. Hitler becomes German Chancellor.

1935

The Jarrow March in England draws attention to high unemployment.

China versus Japan

AD 1905

Japan's push towards industrialization enabled it to wage a successful war against (non-industrialized) China in the 1930s. In 1937 the Chinese attempted to oust the Japanese from Manchuria, a Chinese province which had been under Japanese influence since 1905, and this provoked the Japanese into invading and occupying eastern China. The fighting continued until the end of the Second World War.

January 1932: As the Japanese bombard Shanghai, residents flee in panic.

In the first three decades of the twentieth century, Japan's population grew rapidly as the country industrialized. That industrialization depended on Japan being able to sell products to markets. With the Great Depression, those foreign markets imploded; many of Japan's factories ceased production.

China chose this moment to try to reclaim Manchuria, a Chinese province which Japan had taken in 1905. An attempt to destroy a railway line in Manchuria led to a Japanese occupation of the Manchurian city of Mukden in 1931. The Japanese set up a state there, called Manchuko, the following year. It was officially ruled by the last of the Chinese emperors, Puyi, but he was no more than a puppet king.

TIME LINE	40,000BC	10,000	5000	4000	500	AD1	200	40

The Chinese Civil War between Nationalists and Communists was still raging, but the two sides came together on the outbreak of the Chinese-Japanese War in 1937. Japan attacked a number of Chinese cities – Shanghai, Beijing, Tianjin and Nanjing. Because the Japanese had industrialised, they were able to manufacture more advanced weaponry than the Chinese, which is how they were able to conquer huge areas relatively easily. Among other innovations, the Japanese developed an armoured car, which was halfway between a car and a tank. Within a year Japan had gained control of most of eastern China and Chiang Kai-shek had to leave Nanjing to set up a new capital at Chongqing in Sichuan province. Here they were supported by supplies from Britain and America.

Mao Zedong and his Communist force controlled north-west China, which was free of Japanese control. As the Japanese moved westwards, Soviet troops stopped them.

The Chinese-Japanese War went on to become part of the general War in the Pacific, until the general cessation of hostilities at the end of the Second World War in 1945.

CHRONOLOGY OF EVENTS
AD 1905 – 1945

1905

Japan takes Manchuria and declares Korea a Japanese protectorate.

1931

The Japanese occupy the Manchurian city of Mukden. League of Nations debate on Japan's aggression. Anti-Chinese riots in Korea.

1932

The Japanese set up a state called Manchuko in Manchuria, with former Chinese emperor Puyi as chief executive.

7 July 1937

The Chinese-Japanese War begins when Japan invades north-east China.

28 July 1937

Japanese troops seize Beijing and Tianjin.

11 Nov 1937

Japanese troops seize Shanghai.

5 Dec 1937

Japan takes Nanjing, killing 250,000 Chinese.

1 Jun 1938

The Chinese break embankments along the Yellow River, halting the Japanese advance with water.

1945

The Chinese-Japanese War ends with the general cessation of hostilities at the end of the Second World War.

Science & Technology, 1900–1960

AD 1900

OVERVIEW ❖ OVERVIEW ❖ OVERVIEW ❖ OVERVIEW ❖ OVERVIEW

Plastics made a range of cheap products, including clothing, available to a larger number of people. Developments in transport included long-distance flight, the invention of the jet engine and the birth of rocket science. Transistors made smaller and more powerful computers possible.

A great technological leap was made with the development of plastics, first Bakelite, which was rigid, then a whole range of plastics with various properties, including alkathene, polythene, nylon, polyester. Partly prompted by shortages in the Second World War, many common household goods were made from plastic. Plastic made possible the invention of the ballpoint pen, by Lazlo Biro, in 1938. The invention of synthetic fibres allowed clothing to be mass produced at prices that many more people could afford. Rayon, initially called artificial silk, was use for dress-making as early as the 1920s. The first nylon stockings were sold in the USA in 1939.

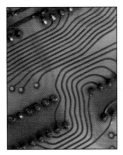

The silicon chip.

In transport, there were huge steps forward. In 1919, Alcock and Brown made the first non-stop transatlantic flight. In 1937,

TIME LINE	40,000BC	10,000	5000	4000	500	AD1	200	40

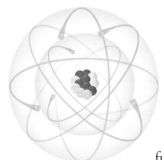

Ernest Rutherford, in 1919, discovered the possibility of splitting the atom. His findings were used in the development of the atomic bomb.

Frank Whittle built the first aircraft jet engine. In 1926, the first liquid-fuelled rocket was launched in the USA, the start of a long process that led to the Moon landings.

The invention of the transistor in 1948 by the Bell Telephone Company was a major breakthrough in many branches of sound engineering; it enabled sound to be amplified with a tiny device. This brought about a revolution in electronics, with smaller and neater radios, record players and television sets.

Computers too were developed. The first entirely electronic computer was used in 1940 for breaking German codes. Transistors made it possible to build smaller and more powerful computers after 1948. By the 1960s, these had become fairly sophisticated, but still very unwieldy. The development of the silicon chip made it possible to pack complex electronic circuitry into a very small space, and computers could be made much smaller. This led the way to the first generation of home computers.

In 1919, Ernest Rutherford discovered that it was possible to split the atom. This led on, through the work of Enrico Fermi in the 1930s, to the development of the atomic bombs that were dropped on Hiroshima and Nagasaki to bring the Second World War to an end. It also led to the development shortly afterwards of nuclear power stations.

Albert Einstein's work in Physics was also exploited in the development of the atomic bomb.

CHRONOLOGY OF EVENTS
AD 1919 – 1981

1919

Alcock and Brown made the first non-stop transatlantic flight. Robert Goddard devises the first two-stage rocket. Ernest Rutherford discovers that nuclear fission is possible.

1926

The first liquid-fuelled rocket is launched.

1935

Wallace Carothers invents nylon.

1937

Enrico Fermi tests nuclear fission. Frank Whittle builds the first aircraft jet engine.

1938

Lazlo Biro invents the ballpoint pen.

1939

USA: The first nylon stockings go on sale.

1940

The first entirely electronic computer is used for breaking German codes.

1948

The transistor is invented by the Bell Telephone Company.

1954

The first atomic power station, at Obninsk near Moscow, begins producing electricity. The first practical silicon transistors are made by Texas Instruments.

1959

Computers are used in business offices.

1981

The first generation of IBM home computers.

The Second World War (1): War Breaks Out

AD 1939

The main causes of the Second World War were the militarist fascist regimes in Germany, Italy and Soviet Union, and the humiliation of Germany under the terms of the Versailles Peace Settlement. These countries, and Japan, all wanted to enlarge their territories. Hitler's blitzkrieg invasions of neighbouring states were extremely successful, and within a few months in 1939 and 1940 much of Europe was under fascist rule.

Adolf Hitler
1889–1945.

The Second World War was caused indirectly by the harsh and humiliating terms of the Versailles Peace Settlement, which made many Germans welcome the aggressive militarism of National Socialism. The war was fought between the Axis Powers, Germany, Italy and Japan, and the Allied Powers, which included the British Empire, France, America and the Soviet Union (now the Russian Federation). Nazi Germany was expansionist, wanting more territory. Italy and Japan wanted more territory too.

The first significant step was the German invasion of Czechoslovakia (now Czech Republic and Slovakia). Italy had taken land in East Africa and Albania. Japan had invaded eastern China. The German leader, Hitler, thought that because the rest of Europe had turned a blind eye to his invasion of Czechoslovakia he could take Poland too. But when he did so on 1 September 1939, Britain and France intervened, declaring war on Germany on 3 September. The Soviet leader, Joseph Stalin (1879–1953), another

TIME LINE	40,000BC	10,000	5000	4000	500	AD1	200	40

German troops advance into a burning forest during the 'Blitzkrieg'.

military dictator but of a communist state, had made a non-aggression pact with Germany, but he immediately ordered Russian troops to invade Poland from the east on 17 September 1939.

Poland had a huge army but it was not equipped with modern weapons; the country was soon defeated and split between Germany and Russia. Hitler's invasion method was a technique called 'blitzkrieg', lightning war. This involved a surprise attack with huge numbers of tanks to overwhelm any ground defences. Aircraft moved in to bomb any remaining defences, then infantry moved into annihilate any pockets of resistance. Blitzkrieg worked very successfully against country after country.

Hitler's next move was to try to take Scandinavia. Following Stalin's invasion of Finland in November 1939, Hitler ordered the invasion of Denmark and Norway in March 1940. In May, German troops invaded Belgium. With so much of Europe now under Fascist rule, and with the USA still safely uninvolved in the war, Hitler thought it was safe to invade Britain.

The Second World War (2): the War in Europe Ends
AD 1945

OVERVIEW ❖ OVERVIEW ❖ OVERVIEW ❖ OVERVIEW ❖ OVERVIEW

Hitler's plan to invade Britain came to nothing, thanks to Britain's victory in the air at the Battle of Britain in 1940. Hitler unwisely opened an Eastern Front with Russia. The entry of America into the war as a result of the unprovoked Japanese attack on Pearl Harbour was decisive, and the days of the great dictators were numbered.

The Battle of Britain began on 10 July 1940. Britain was helped greatly by having an inspirational war leader in Winston Churchill (1874–1965), and in being an island. Hitler was unable to land large numbers of tanks as there was no land frontier for them to swarm across. British beaches were lined with anti-tank defences. The attack by the Luftwaffe, the German air force, was met by strong resistance from the RAF, the British air force, through the summer and autumn of 1940 over the skies of Kent and Sussex. On 31 October, after losing over 1700 German planes over south-east England, Hitler abandoned his plan to invade Britain. Instead, in April 1941, Germany invaded Greece and Yugoslavia to help the Italians.

The Japanese attack on Pearl Harbour in Hawaii in 1941 brought the Americans into the war, not just in the Pacific but in Europe too; this sealed the fate of the dictators. After that, Hitler's fortunes

Sir Winston Churchill, 1874–1965.

TIME LINE	40,000BC	10,000	5000	4000	500	AD1	200	4(

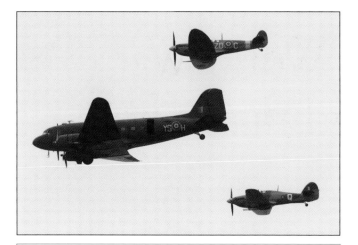

A Battle of Britain Memorial Flight.

10 July 1940

The Battle of Britain begins.

31 Oct 1940

The Battle of Britain ends with the RAF defeating the German Luftwaffe. Hitler abandons his planned invasion of Britain.

22 Jun 1941

Operation Barbarossa. Hitler invades Russia, unwisely opening a second front on the East.

13 Sep 1942–2 Feb 1943

Battle of Stalingrad. Heavy German losses.

23 Oct–4 Nov 1942

Battle of El Alamein.

3 Sep 1943

The Italians surrender as British troops invade the Italian mainland. German troops fight on.

6 Jun 1944

The D-Day landings in Normandy began.

28 Jan 1945

Battle of the Bulge. Germans forced back.

30 Apr 1945

Hitler commits suicide in his bunker in Berlin.

went into decline. He unwisely declared war on the Soviet Union in 1941, opening a second front on the East. His goal was the Baku oilfields on the Caspian Sea. The German army was only turned back by fierce Russian resistance at the Battle of Stalingrad in 1943. Losses there severely weakened the German army.

Allied troops in the Middle East and Africa succeeded in taking Iraq, Iran, Syria, Lebanon and Ethiopia. In North Africa, they won the Battle of El Alamein against a combined force of German and Italian troops.

The Allies attacked Italy in early 1944, and gradually, beginning in the south, took it from the fascists. Meanwhile the Allies were planning to retake France. The D-Day landings in Normandy began on 6 June 1944. Germany tried a counter-offensive in December 1944, but was forced back in January 1945. Russian troops advanced from the east, eventually reaching Berlin, where Hitler committed suicide on 30 April 1945, shortly after hearing the news that Mussolini had been shot.

The Second World War (3): the War in the Pacific

AD 1941

OVERVIEW ❖ OVERVIEW ❖ OVERVIEW ❖ OVERVIEW ❖ OVERVIEW

The Americans were brought into the Second World War by a surprise Japanese attack on Pearl Harbour in December 1941. Japan invaded territory after territory in south-east Asia, quickly gaining control over a huge area. The Americans won a series of battles in 1942, then slowly recaptured the Japanese-occupied territories.
The Japanese were reluctant to surrender, so the Americans dropped atomic bombs on first one city, Hiroshima, then another, Nagasaki, until they surrendered.

The use of atomic bombs brought the war in the pacific to a sudden end.

Japan's attack on the US naval base at Pearl Harbour in Hawaii opened the war in the Pacific. The surprise attack destroyed four battleships, disabled many others, killed 3,000 servicemen and shocked America into entering the Second World War. On the same day, 7 December 1941, Japan invaded Thailand. Within a few months, Japan had invaded Burma, Singapore, Malaya, the Dutch East Indies (now Malaysia and Indonesia), the Philippines, New Guinea and Hong Kong.

It looked as if Japan would take the whole of the Pacific basin, including Australia. The Americans responded vigorously in 1942, winning major victories at the Battle of the Coral Sea (May), the Battle of Midway (June) and the Battle of Guadalcanal (August). This halted Japanese expansion.

Through 1943 and 1944, the Americans began to recapture the territories occupied by the Japanese. First they recaptured the Gilbert, Marshall, Caroline and Mariana Islands. They were then able to turn these islands into bases from which they could attack Japan itself.

Towards the end of 1944, the Americans began to recapture the Philippines. At the same

TIME LINE	40,000BC	10,000	5000	4000	500	AD1	200	4

time British troops began to retake Burma.

The Allies planned to invade Japan in late 1945, but America feared that the Japanese would slaughter the hundreds of thousands of prisoners-of-war they held and decided to bring the war to a sudden end by a means that continues to be controversial – the bombing of two Japanese cities with atomic bombs. On 6 August, the first atomic bomb was dropped on Hiroshima. Up to 100,000 civilians were killed in the blast; thousands more died later from injuries and radiation sickness. Even this horror did not produce an immediate surrender, so three days later a second bomb was dropped on Nagasaki, with similar effects. Five days later Japan surrendered.

The Second World War formally ended when Japanese leaders signed a statement of surrender on 2 September, 1945.

Japanese memorial to the hundreds of thousands who died in the nuclear attacks in 1945.

CHRONOLOGY OF EVENTS
AD 1941 – 1945

7 Dec 1941

The Japanese surprise attack on Pearl Harbour, a US naval base, destroys four battleships, killing 3,000 servicemen.

8 Dec 1941

USA and UK declare war on Japan.

4–5 Jun 1942

Battle of Midway. US planes sink 4 Japanese aircraft carriers.

7 Aug 1942

Battle of Guadalcanal begins.

1 Nov 1943

American troops land in the Solomon Islands.

29 Jan 1944

American forces launch a series of offensives, retaking one Japanese-occupied Pacific island after another.

17–25 Oct 1944

Battle of Leyte Gulf. The greatest naval battle in history, in which the Americans began to recapture the Philippines. The Americans destroy 4 carriers, 3 battleships, 10 cruisers, 9 destroyers.

6 Aug 1945

The US drops the first atomic bomb on Hiroshima.

9 Aug 1945

A second atomic bomb is dropped on Nagasaki.

2 Sep 1945

Japan formally surrenders.

The End of the British Empire

AD 1947

OVERVIEW ❖ OVERVIEW ❖ OVERVIEW ❖ OVERVIEW ❖ OVERVIEW

Britain's colonies wanted independence, some achieving it early in the twentieth century, others acquiring semi-independent dominion status as a halfway measure. The independence of India – a traumatic episode in 1947 - led the way to independence for most British colonies in the 1960s and 1970s. Many colonies exchanged political colonialism for economic colonialism.

Many of the native peoples in British colonies had always, from the beginning, wanted their independence. By the beginning of the twentieth century the British government had been forced to recognize this and the relationship between Britain and its colonies began to change; some colonies acquired semi-independent status as dominions. Canada, Australia and New Zealand became independent states before the First World War, but remained loyal to the Empire, sending troops to fight alongside Britain in both World Wars. The Irish Free State became a dominion in 1921. By the time of the Imperial Conference of 1926, the dominions were asking for a greater measure of independence; they wanted control over their own foreign policies. In 1931, the Statute of Westminster redefined dominions as 'autonomous communities within the British Empire. . . freely associated as members of the British Commonwealth of Nations'.

In 1945, Attlee's government decided to give India its full independence, within the British Commonwealth. This was difficult to achieve because of political and religious disunity within the Indian subcontinent.

Muslims would not agree to a form of government that put them under Hindu rule. The Muslim leader, Muhammed Ali Jinnah (1876–1948), pressed for a separate Muslim state, and on 14 August, 1947, the British agreed to partition. A Muslim state called Pakistan was created, but it was itself divided into West and East Pakistan, with Jinnah as its first governor general. Millions of Muslims moved from India into East or West Pakistan; millions of Hindus moved from Pakistan into India. There were many religious riots, in which a million

TIME LINE	40,000BC	10,000	5000	4000	500	AD1	200

people were killed. The great campaigner for Indian independence, Mahatma Gandhi, was himself assassinated by a Hindu extremist in 1948.

The next two colonies to achieve full independence were Ceylon (now Sri Lanka) and Burma, both in 1948. Ghana became independent in 1957, and most of the remaining colonies gained their independence in the 1960s and 1970s.

For many ex-colonies the path to freedom was fraught with problems. Some exchanged political colonialism for economic colonialism.

Seated on the Indian Elephant, whose tusks are blunted by the policy of non violence, Gandhi defies the violence of the British Lion.

CHRONOLOGY OF EVENTS
AD 1926 – 1966

1926

Imperial Conference. Dominions ask for more independence.

1931

The phrase 'British Commonwealth of Nations' is introduced.

15 Aug 1947

India is given full independence. Partition into India and West and East Pakistan.

30 Jan 1948

Mahatma Gandhi is assassinated by a Hindu extremist.

1948

Ceylon (now Sri Lanka) and Burma achieve full independence.

1957

Ghana becomes independent.

1959

Singapore becomes independent.

1959

Tanganyika and Sierra Leone become independent.

1962

Jamaica and Uganda become independent.

1964

Malta, Malawi and Zambia become independent.

1965

Gambia becomes independent.

1966

Lesotho becomes independent.

The Cold War

AD 1950

OVERVIEW ❖ OVERVIEW ❖ OVERVIEW ❖ OVERVIEW ❖ OVERVIEW

After the end of the Second World War, the Allies became enemies in a war without open fighting – a propaganda war. The Soviet Union strengthened its hold over eastern Europe, creating a communist empire. America and the Soviet Union threatened each other with stockpiles of nuclear weapons. The Cuba crisis of 1962 was the nearest they came to open warfare, and the Soviet Union backed down. The Cold War ended when, suffering economic collapse in 1989, the Soviet Union agreed to decommission its nuclear missiles. The Soviet Union as a political entity disintegrated in 1991.

In the Second World War, the Soviet Union, Britain and America fought side by side to defeat the Axis Powers, but in the aftermath of war in 1945, they became enemies. This division – a war without fighting – was known as the Cold War. Britain was obliged to side with America, because of America's help in defeating Hitler. In eastern Europe, the Soviet Union gained control of one country after another, in much the same way that Germany had a decade earlier, but this time there was no intervention. The threat of nuclear war was too great.

The two sides threatened each other by maintaining stockpiles of nuclear weapons. The West formed NATO, the North Atlantic Treaty Organization, an alliance against the communist powers. The Soviet Union formed the Warsaw Pact, an alliance of East European communist states. There was resistance to the Soviets from within eastern Europe, in Hungary in 1956 and Czechoslovakia in 1968, but Moscow sent in troops to suppress rebellion and strengthened its hold.

The war of words between the great powers often seemed about to erupt into war, but open fighting never broke out. The nearest they came to war was in 1962, when Soviet missiles were shipped to Cuba.

TIME LINE	40,000BC	10,000	5000	4000	500	AD1	200	40

US President John F. Kennedy (1917–1963) insisted that the Soviet leader, Nikita Khrushchev (1894–1971), must back down; he did.

The arms race was extremely expensive as well as dangerous, and discussions about disarmament started in 1969. In 1989, when the Soviet Union faced economic collapse, the two sides agreed to destroy their medium-range nuclear missiles. The end of the Cold War came when the Soviet Union disintegrated politically; President Yeltsin (1931–) ended the Communist Party's power in August 1991 after 74 years. In September the independence of Lithuania, Latvia and Estonia was recognized. Other republics broke away from the former Soviet Union, leaving a smaller non-communist Russian Federation.

CHRONOLOGY OF EVENTS
AD 1946 – 1991

5 Mar 1946

Churchill makes his 'Iron Curtain' speech, the formal beginning of the Cold War.

4 Apr 1949

The West forms NATO, an alliance against the communist powers.

14 May 1955

The Soviet Union forms the Warsaw Pact, allying East European communist states.

17 Aug 1961

The Berlin Wall is built.

22–28 Oct 1962

The Cuban missile crisis.

1969

Discussion about disarmament starts.

10 Nov 1989

Demolition of the Berlin Wall begins.

2 Dec 1989

Presidents Bush and Gorbachev declare the Cold War over.

29 Aug 1991

President Yeltsin ends the rule of the Communist Party in Russia.

The flags of the NATO members.
Right: NATO's emblem.

The Space Race

AD 1957

OVERVIEW ❖ OVERVIEW ❖ OVERVIEW ❖ OVERVIEW ❖ OVERVIEW

Second World War rocketry was developed to make manned space travel possible, previously a dream of science fiction writers. The 'space race' was fuelled by the Cold War rivalry between the Soviet Union and the USA. Initially the Soviets were more successful, launching satellites and Moon probes, but it was the Americans who put men on the Moon. Recent projects have focused on unmanned probes that can collect data from all round the solar system and beyond.

The rocket science developed during the Second World War, especially by the Germans who built the V-2, made it possible for scientists and politicians to contemplate the possibility of manned space travel. It had been a dream of science fiction writers like Jules Verne and H. G. Wells, but now it seemed to be achievable. The drive to make it a reality came from the Cold War rivalry between the Soviets and the Americans; a success would be a propaganda triumph, and the new technology would help improve weaponry.

The Soviet scientists were initially spectacularly successful, launching a tiny satellite, Sputnik 1, in 1957. Sputnik 2, launched the same year, was manned by a dog called Laika. The dog could not be returned to Earth, and was humanely poisoned by its last feed. This turned out to be a propaganda failure, as many people felt sorry for the dog. The Luna 2

TIME LINE	40,000BC	10,000	5000	4000	500	AD1	200

probe was more successful, in showing that the Russians could reach the Moon. Yuri Gagarin, a Russian again, was the first man in space, in 1961.

In that year, President Kennedy boasted that the USA would land a man on the Moon by the end of the decade. He was right. In 1969, Neil Armstrong and Edwin Aldrin landed on the Moon (Apollo 11). The Soviet scientists were able to cap that achievement in 1971, by sending two probes to Mars.

A hint that the Cold War might be thawing came in 1975, when the US Apollo and Soviet Soyuz spacecraft docked (linked together) while in orbit. The Soviet space station (a long-term orbiting satellite) was launched in 1986, and it has been visited by non-Soviet scientists.

Recent projects have concentrated on unmanned probes sent to various parts of the solar system to collect information about other planets. In 1986, the Pioneer spacecraft left the solar system altogether. One of the latest ventures has been the launching of the Hubble Space Telescope in 1990. This has been able to collect a great deal of new astronomical information about the universe outside our own galaxy, unimpeded by interference from the Earth's atmosphere.

CHRONOLOGY OF EVENTS
AD 1957 – 1990

4 Oct 1957

Sputnik 1 is launched, the first artificial satellite.

12 Apr 1961

Yuri Gagarin is the first person in space.

18 Oct 1967

Soviet Venera 4 lands on Venus.

21–27 Dec 1968

Apollo 8 makes the first crewed mission to the Moon, completing 10 orbits before returning to Earth.

16–24 Jul 1969

Apollo 11. Neil Armstrong and Edwin Aldrin land on the Moon.

13 Apr 1970

Apollo 13. Moon landing aborted because of explosion in Command module.

1971

Soviet scientists send two probes to Mars and launch Salyut 1 space station.

1975

US Apollo and Soviet Soyuz spacecraft dock while in orbit.

28 Jan 1986

Explosion of space shuttle Challenger leads to suspension of shuttle flights.

19 Feb 1986

The Soviet Mir space station is launched.

24 Apr 1990

The Hubble Space Telescope is launched.

South-East Asia: the Many Small Wars

AD 1950

OVERVIEW ❖ OVERVIEW ❖ OVERVIEW ❖ OVERVIEW ❖ OVERVIEW

The colonial powers in Europe expected to re-establish the pre-war situation in countries that had been invaded by the Japanese. The native people had been changed by their experience of the Second World War, and were no longer prepared to be dominated by foreign states. They fought for their independence. The freedom-fighters also fought among themselves, communists against capitalists. This drew the great powers – China, the Soviet Union, the USA – into the conflict and greatly increased the misery of the native people.

South-East Asia in 1950 had been badly damaged economically by the Japanese invasion. Businesses and farms were in ruins. The fighting continued, partly because the native peoples wanted to be free of outside interference, free of the old colonial masters. France, Britain and the Netherlands wanted to hang on to these potentially rich territories, and expected to go back to the way things had been before the Second World War. But the experience of war had changed many people's attitudes, both in Asia and in Europe.

Separate wars broke out in Indonesia, Malaysia, Burma, the Philippines, Vietnam, Laos, Thailand and Cambodia. These wars for independence were often made more complicated by in-fighting between various rival factions among the freedom-fighters. Some were

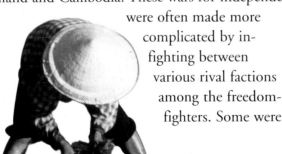

TIME LINE	40,000BC	10,000	5000	4000	500	AD1	200	4

Vietnamese farmers plant rice (below left), while an American soldier plants mines (right).

communist, some capitalist. Korea was divided into a communist north and a capitalist south. The situation became even more complicated when the Soviet Union and America joined in, seeing this as an arena for weapons-testing and a safe way of testing their real enemy's strength. In 1950 China decided to join in, helping the communist North Koreans with troops, so America sent in troops to help the South Koreans; 3 million Koreans were killed or made homeless before the Korean War ended in 1953. It was in the Korean War that helicopters were used on a big scale (for moving troops across difficult terrain such as mountains or forests) for the first time.

The biggest and most controversial war in South-East Asia was the Vietnam War (1964–1975). As in Korea, the North was backed by communists, and the Americans backed the South, arriving in 1965. This was a savage war, with many atrocities, some committed by American soldiers. Forests were sprayed with chemicals to kill the vegetation that provided cover for the enemy. Many land mines were planted. Large numbers of harmless civilians were killed in crossfire. Many were made homeless and fled across the borders into neighbouring countries. The Vietnam War spread to Laos in 1971. The American government finally decided to give up the Vietnam War in 1975, largely because of pressure at home from the families and friends of American soldiers who had lost their lives. Communist forces took over the whole of Vietnam; communist Pathet-Lao forces took over Laos.

Unfortunately, the interference of the great powers only prolonged the wars and added greatly to the misery of the ordinary people of South-East Asia.

CHRONOLOGY OF EVENTS
AD 1950 – 1975

28 Jun 1950

North Koreans capture Seoul in South Korea. The South Korean army is annihilated.

1 Jul 1950

First UN troops arrive in Korea.

26 Sep 1950

UN troops recapture Seoul.

27 Jul 1953

Korean War ends.

1964

Vietnam War begins.

1965

US troops arrive, backing South Vietnam.

29 Jun 1966

US begins bombing Hanoi.
UK condemns bombing of cities.

1971

The Vietnam War spreads to Laos.

1975

America decides to give up the Vietnam War.
Communist forces take over
the whole of Vietnam.
The Vietnam War ends.

Art

AD 1900

Artists in the twentieth century were freed by photography to explore their inner visions and use paint, stone and other media for self-expression rather than mere representation. Expressionism followed impressionism, abstract art followed cubism. Later there was a reaction to abstract art; most people looking at art wanted to know what it was 'about'. Above all, there was a tremendous variety of personal style, which owes a huge debt to an earlier, Romantic, view of the artist.

Pablo Picasso (1881–1973) was one of the key figures in twentieth century art. In 1907 he initiated cubism, in which the subject matter was reduced to geometric shapes. The first cubist painting was *Les Demoiselles d'Avignon*. His 1937 painting *Guernica* shows the ruthless savagery of the town's destruction by German bombers, and remains the most powerful anti-war painting.

Marc Chagall (1889–1985) produced intensely personal paintings that included a medley of animals, objects, people and dreams from Chagall's past life. The word 'surrealist' was coined to describe his work.

Paul Klee (1879–1940) was also called a surrealist, but his small-scale and fanciful pictures are more whimsical than that. He was a witty and self-effacing artist. He seemed to want to give the impression that his pictures, such as *Twittering Machine*, are no more than doodles.

Above: Picasso's *Woman Weeping*, October 1937.
Right: Henry Moore's bronze sculpture, *King and Queen*, 1952–3.

Henry Moore (1898–1986) was one of the most powerful and original sculptors of his

TIME LINE	40,000BC	10,000	5000	4000	500	AD1	200	40

age. He produced figures and groups of figures in a semi-abstract style that reflected the swelling forms of the English landscape. They were also influenced by primitive African art. His best-known sculpture is the *Madonna and Child* in St Matthew's Church, Northampton.

Jackson Pollock (1912–1956)

Jackson Pollock (1912–1956) was the first 'action' painter. He produced his first drip painting in 1947, developing the technique with increasing violence and on an increasing scale. His paintings are near-animal in feeling; some feel they could actually have been painted by chimpanzees.

David Hockney (1937–)

David Hockney (1937–) brings the century back to representational art in a refreshing way, simplifying images into flat shapes. Hockney's pictures have a freshness and innocence that is extremely popular. He also designs imaginative and colourful stage sets, such as *The Magic Flute* at Glyndebourne in 1978.

1907	Pablo Picasso: *Les Demoiselles d'Avignon.*
1912	Picasso: *The Violin.*
1914	Paul Klee: *The Creator.*
1937	Picasso: *Guernica.*
1919	Marc Chagall : *Anywhere Out of the World.*
1919	Klee: *Dream Birds.*
1922	Klee: *Twittering Machine.*
1929	Chagall: *Love Idyll.*
1930	Chagall: *Lovers in the Lilacs.*
1936	Henry Moore: *Two Forms.*
1938	Moore: *Recumbent Figures.*
1943	Jackson Pollock: *The She-Wolf.*
1945	Moore: *Family Group.*
1946	Picasso: *Faun Playing the Pipe.*
1947	Pollock: *Full Fathom Five.*
1950	Pollock: *Autumn Rhythm.*
1950	Picasso: *The Goat.*
1953	Moore: *King and Queen.*
1961	David Hockney: *Typhoo Tea.*
1970	Hockney: *Mr and Mrs Ossie Clark and Percy.*
1971	Hockney: *Rubber Ring Floating in a Swimming Pool.*
1978	Hockney: *Sets for The Magic Flute.*

The Sixties & Social Change

AD 1960

OVERVIEW ❖ OVERVIEW ❖ OVERVIEW ❖ OVERVIEW ❖ OVERVIEW

The Sixties were a time of student protest, and also a time of anxiety about accelerating population growth and the widening gap between rich and poor countries. The women's movement led to greater equality between men and women in pay, recruitment and promotion. There were also still countries where gross injustices went on, such as South Africa, where the apartheid doctrine (separate development for black and white people) continued.

Many young people in the 1960s took part in protest movements. Some called for a social revolution based on peace, freedom and even free love. Some wanted more say in the structure of their university courses. Some protested about the dangerous bullying tactics of America towards the Soviet Union during the Cuba crisis. Protest songs were popular, and singers such as Bob Dylan and Joan Baez acquired cult status. There were also larger scale changes.

Accelerating population growth, especially in the poorer countries, alarmed people and popularized the spread of birth control. The gap between rich and poor countries widened. In the rich countries, the power of the press and television increased and so did the power of advertising. A consumer society developed, preoccupied with fashion, style and quality of life.

In the rich countries, people moved around more as they changed jobs. In the new 'permissive society' people changed partners more, and divorce became more common. The status

A typical Sixties girl in a white mini-skirted outfit and sunglasses, window shopping in Carnaby St.

TIME LINE	40,000BC	10,000	5000	4000	500	AD1	200	4

A handbill, published in England, encourages consumers to boycott South African goods to demonstrate their opposition to the apartheid regime in South Africa.

Boycott SOUTH AFRICAN Goods MARCH 1ST to 31ST 1960

CALLED BY the African, Indian and Coloured Peoples of South Africa, including the South African National Congress Movement, and by the South African Liberal Party.

IN GREAT BRITAIN BACKED BY
● Christian Action
● Co-operative Organisations
● Committee of African Organisations
● The Labour Party
● The Liberal Party
● National Council for Civil Liberties
● Student Organisations
● The Trades Union Congress and many other organisations

An opportunity for British people to support the majority of the South African people in protest against:—
● Apartheid and Racial Discrimination
● The Treason Trials
● The ghettos of the Group Areas Act
● Poverty wages for Africans

of women changed too, with a greater degree of equality; more young women opted to have jobs or even professional careers, rather than being mere housewives as many of their mothers had been. Women demanded equal pay with men and an end to sexual discrimination. New laws ensured that the demand for 'Women's Liberation' was met.

The rights of children were increasingly considered. It was seen that, as far as possible, they should have the same rights as adults. In schools, corporal punishment, which had been a normal part of schooling in many countries, was banned. It was recognized that children had the right not to be assaulted.

Side by side with these trends, there were still countries where profoundly destructive racial prejudice held sway. Apartheid, the doctrine of separate development for black and white people, was still a powerful force in South Africa. Blacks and whites were not allowed to use the same public toilets; every aspect of their lives was segregated. A great deal of pressure was applied on South Africa by other countries to do away with this destructive and degrading doctrine, but apartheid would not be abolished until 1990.

CHRONOLOGY OF EVENTS
AD 1960 – 1970

1960
The Pill becomes available in the USA, and in the UK the following year.

1963
UK Robbins Report marks the start of a 10-year expansion in higher education.

1964
US civil rights campaigner Martin Luther King is awarded the Nobel Peace Prize.

1965
Demonstration against Vietnam War at University of Michigan.

1966
US National Organization of Women set up. In UK seven new universities and 30 polytechnics are created. In the Vatican the office of Inquisitor and the list of prohibited books are abolished.

1967
Race riots in 70 US cities. UK Sexual Offences Act legalizes homosexual acts between consenting adults.

1968
Violent student demonstrations in France, UK and USA. South African Council of Churches condemns racial segregation as 'hostile to Christianity'.

1969
UK Divorce Reform Act permits divorce after 2 years' separation, both parties consenting.

1970
Equal Pay Act in UK makes discrimination in wages on basis of sex illegal.

Literature

AD 1900

In the literature of the early twentieth century we begin to see a gradual movement away from the realist and conservative style of the nineteenth century novelists and playwrights, towards a more daring approach to writing. The novels of James Joyce and D.H.Lawrence challenged traditional assumptions, writing about sensitive subjects in direct and provocative ways. Both authors had some works censored or banned.

James Joyce (1882–1941)

Joyce corresponded with Ibsen, and was influenced by Dante and Yeats. He was highly regarded as a writer well before his key novel, *Ulysses* (1922), was published. It drew on ideas from psychology and produced violent reactions, revolutionizing the development of the novel. A second great novel appeared in 1939, *Finnegan's Wake*, which is full of witty word-play and obscure references to all sorts of subjects from Wagner to local history.

George Bernard Shaw (1856–1950)

Shaw, like his great European contemporaries, Ibsen and Chekhov, was interested in making his plays more realistic, dealing with major social issues of the day. Reading Karl Marx converted him to socialism. He also wrote witty and mischievous music reviews for the papers. He wrote many plays, such as the philosophical comedy *Man and Superman* (1902). He is probably best known for his 'anti-romantic comedy' *Pygmalion* (1913), which was adapted as a musical, *My Fair Lady*, in 1956.

| TIME LINE | 40,000BC | 10,000 | 5000 | 4000 | 500 | AD1 | 200 | 4(|

Thomas Mann (1875–1955)

Mann's novel about a TB sanatorium in Davos, *The Magic Mountain*, won him the Nobel Prize in 1924. His greatest work was *Doktor Faustus* (1947), which deals with the tragic life of a fictitious composer and the disintegration of Germany through two world wars.

Samuel Beckett (1906–89)

Beckett was for a time James Joyce's secretary, and shared his preoccupation with language. His ground-breaking play was *Waiting for Godot* (1956), which was enormously popular, in spite of its depressing view of the human condition, with its futile hopes, philosophies and endeavours.

D. H. Lawrence (1885–1930)

Lawrence specialized in novels that explored married (and unmarried) love, in books such as *The Rainbow* (1915) and *Women in Love* (1921). He was vigorously anti-Victorian in his attitudes, wanting people to be franker about their physical nature. There is no humour in his books, but his descriptive writing is superb.

John Updike (1932–)

Updike has a continuing career as a journalist, but his main reputation rests on his novels. Best known are his Rabbit books, about the life of a car salesman: *Rabbit, Run* (1960), *Rabbit Redux* (1971), *Rabbit is Rich* (1981) and *Rabbit at Rest* (1996).

CHRONOLOGY OF EVENTS
AD 1900 – 1995

1900	Anton Chekhov: *Uncle Vanya*.
1904	Anton Chekhov: *The Cherry Orchard*.
1912	George Bernard Shaw: *Androcles and the Lion*.
1913	Thomas Mann: *Death in Venice*.
1915	D. H. Lawrence: *The Rainbow*.
1919	George Bernard Shaw: *Heartbreak House*.
1921	D. H. Lawrence: *Women in Love*.
1922	James Joyce: *Ulysses*.
1923	George Bernard Shaw: *Saint Joan*.
1924	W. B. Yeats: *A Vision*.
1924	Thomas Mann: *The Magic Mountain*.
1939	James Joyce: *Finnegan's Wake*.
1947	Thomas Mann: *Doktor Faustus*.
1954	Thomas Mann: *Confessions of the Confidence Trickster Felix Krull*.
1956	Samuel Beckett: *Waiting for Godot*.
1957	Samuel Beckett: *Endgame*.
1960	John Updike: *Rabbit, Run*.
1995	John Updike: *Rabbit at Rest*.

Environmental Awareness
AD 1970

OVERVIEW ❖ OVERVIEW ❖ OVERVIEW ❖ OVERVIEW ❖ OVERVIEW

The late twentieth century saw a significant shift towards a feeling of responsibility towards the environment. People became aware that agriculture and industry were creating large-scale pollution and that natural resources were running out. There were major campaigns to save the rain forests in Brazil and the whales – both in danger of extinction.

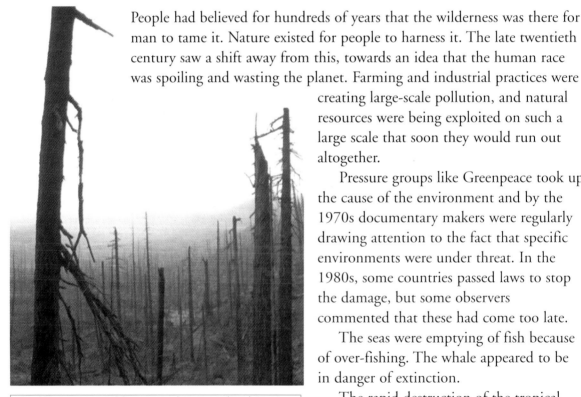

Acid Rain is caused by toxic substances dissolving into the air's moisture and falling as rain. It kills vegetation and the organsims which feed on it.

People had believed for hundreds of years that the wilderness was there for man to tame it. Nature existed for people to harness it. The late twentieth century saw a shift away from this, towards an idea that the human race was spoiling and wasting the planet. Farming and industrial practices were creating large-scale pollution, and natural resources were being exploited on such a large scale that soon they would run out altogether.

Pressure groups like Greenpeace took up the cause of the environment and by the 1970s documentary makers were regularly drawing attention to the fact that specific environments were under threat. In the 1980s, some countries passed laws to stop the damage, but some observers commented that these had come too late.

The seas were emptying of fish because of over-fishing. The whale appeared to be in danger of extinction.

The rapid destruction of the tropical rain forests, especially in South America,

TIME LINE	40,000BC	10,000	5000	4000	500	AD1	200	40

Deforestation – over half of the world's forests were cut down during the twentieth century.

was a major concern. Forests were being cut down for the sake of the valuable timber and to make highways, so that colonists could drive in and clear more of the forest for farms. The soil turned out to be infertile in many places, so yet more land was cleared. The Brazilian government ran up a huge international debt and wanted to pay it off by exploiting the mineral resources beneath the forest and the hydro-electric potential of the river system that ran through it.

Major accidents such as Three Mile Island in the USA in 1979 and Chernobyl in Russia in 1986 showed people how dangerous the new technology was.

The discovery in the late 1970s and 1980s that a hole was opening in the ozone layer alerted many people to the fact that industrial pollution was capable of having a global impact.

In many countries, it was seen that recycling some materials, such as glass, cans and paper, would make good sense, environmentally and economically.

CHRONOLOGY OF EVENTS
AD 1961 – 1989

1961

World Wildlife Fund founded.

1971

Greenpeace is founded.

1976

Release of dioxin from a pesticide plant at Seveso kills domestic and farm animals. Evidence of ozone thinning over Antarctica.

1979

Major accident at Three Mile Island nuclear power station in the USA.

1985

An Antarctic 'ozone hole' is identified.

1986

Major accident at Chernobyl nuclear power station in Russia.

1987

International agreement limits use of CFCs.

1989

Convention on International Trade in Endangered Species agrees on a total ban on trading in ivory.

Collapse of the Soviet Union & the End of the Cold War

AD 1991

OVERVIEW ❖ OVERVIEW ❖ OVERVIEW ❖ OVERVIEW ❖ OVERVIEW

By the 1980s the Soviet Union had become severely economically weakened by the Cold War arms race. President Gorbachev of the Soviet Union asked for friendship with the West and introduced a programme of reform. This led to a long-frustrated demand for freedom from some of the Warsaw Pact states, and the collapse of the Soviet Union in 1991. This brought the Cold War to an end.

The Soviet Union was economically weak in the 1980s, weakened partly by the space race and the arms race of the Cold War. There was discontent among the Soviet people. When Mikhail Gorbachev became Soviet leader in 1985 he tried to make the country more efficient. He recognized that collective farms were inefficient and introduced privatization. The keywords of his policies were 'glasnost' (openness) and 'perestroika' (economic reform). The Soviet Union could not afford to maintain huge stockpiles of weapons, so Gorbachev decided to call for an end to the Cold War.

Mikhail Gorbachev, Soviet leader 1985–1991.

These reforms were welcomed by most Soviet people, but they ignited unexpected demands for freedom. The Baltic states – Latvia, Lithuania and Estonia – asked for independence from control by the Communist party. Georgia wanted the same. Gorbachev's reforms were leading to the disintegration of the USSR, so in 1991 a powerful group of politicians tried to take over, but failed.

TIME LINE	40,000BC	10,000	5000	4000	500	AD1	200	4

A patrol guard steadies a civilian by holding her arm as she sits with her two companions on the Berlin Wall.

Instead the old Soviet Union was abolished at the end of 1991, and replaced by a looser alliance of independent states. Gorbachev resigned and was succeeded by Boris Yeltsin.

The swift collapse of the Soviet Union sent shock waves throughout eastern Europe, which had been dominated by Moscow for several decades. The Berlin Wall, built in 1961, was demolished in 1989, symbolizing the end of the division of Germany into a capitalist West and a communist East; the two parts of Germany were shortly afterwards reunited in 1990. Although most Germans welcomed this, the cost to West Germany of modernizing East German industry was very great .

In eastern Europe communist power was challenged and in many cases replaced by liberal Western-style regimes. As early as 1980, an organization called Solidarity was formed in Poland to campaign for workers' rights and freedom from communist party control. Initially it was outlawed and its leader Lech Walesa was arrested, but by 1989 Solidarity was officially recognized and Walesa became President of Poland.

CHRONOLOGY OF EVENTS
AD 1989 – 1991

2 Dec 1989

Presidents Bush and Gorbachev declare the Cold War to be over.

11 Feb 1990

Lithuania declares intention to secede from Soviet Union.

25 Feb 1990

Gorbachev sends tanks into Vilnius, capital of Lithuania, to discourage calls for independence.

4–8 May 1990

Latvia and Estonia declare intention to secede from Soviet Union.

June–July 1990

Uzbekistan declares independence. Ukrainian government votes for independence.

14 Aug 1990

Gorbachev restores citizenship to exiled dissidents.

2 Oct 1990

Germany is formally reunified.

9 Feb–3 Mar 1991

Lithuania, Estonia and Latvia vote in favour of independence.

12 Jun 1991

Boris Yeltsin becomes first leader of Russian Federation.

29 Aug 1991

President Yeltsin ends the rule of the Communist Party in Russia.

The Population Explosion: Unfounded Fears?

AD 1970

OVERVIEW ❖ OVERVIEW ❖ OVERVIEW ❖ OVERVIEW ❖ OVERVIEW

The number of people on the Earth has been growing faster and faster in the last 200 years. This alarmed many people in the 1960s. Some think that the world will soon be over-populated and that there will be famine and population collapse. But people are resourceful and new strains of rice and wheat and new farming methods have meant that food production has increased much faster than the population. The fear of a 'population explosion' was unjustified.

The human population of the world has grown rapidly in the last 200 years. It took the whole history of mankind to reach the one billion level in 1810. By 1930, this had doubled; by 1975 it had quadrupled to 4 billion. This increasing rate worried many people.

Thanks to improved nutrition, sanitation and health care, many more babies survive infancy. The continuing high birth rate and falling death rate is creating a rapid population increase in many countries, especially in Latin America, Africa and Asia.

China is the world's most populated country. It holds over 1 billion people, one-sixth of the entire world's population.

When famine and rapid population growth coincided in India in the 1960s, Stanford biologist Paul Ehrlich jumped to the conclusion that the two were connected. Ehrlich warned of the danger of population collapse.

The economist Julian Simon thought Ehrlich was exaggerating and in 1980 won a bet with Ehrlich that the price of certain resources would actually fall. Ehrlich clung to his

TIME LINE	40,000BC	10,000	5000	4000	500	AD1	200	4

conviction that human population would outstrip the Earth's carrying capacity. Ehrlich's background as a biologist led him to compare people, misleadingly, with fruit flies. When fruit flies find a bunch of bananas they gorge and multiply; when the bananas are used up, the flies die.

Ehrlich overlooked the fact that people are flexible and inventive. New technologies can be invented to produce more food. New strains of wheat and rice have been made to yield five times as much grain. World population may be growing steeply, but so also is food production. The grain harvest for the whole world in 1950 was 631 million tonnes. By 1986 this had grown to 1650 million tonnes. The population had grown 1.9 times during that period, but grain production had grown 2.6 times – more than enough to feed the extra people. In the last decade of the twentieth century, food production increased another 24 percent, once again outstripping population growth. There is more than enough food to go round.

In the 1990s, it was realised that countries with high female literacy rates have low birth rates. The key to bringing down the birth rate is the education of women. This breakthrough has led many to hope that world population may not be too high in a hundred years' time, after all.

The search for work and employment opportunites have brought more and more people to the towns and cities, which are now becoming increasingly over-crowded.

CHRONOLOGY OF EVENTS
AD 1810 – 1990

1810

The world's population reaches 1 billion.

1930

The world's population reaches 2 billion.

1950

The grain harvest for the world is 631 million tonnes.

1968

Famine in Biafra, Nigeria. Paul Ehrlich's book The Population Bomb warns of the danger of world population collapse.

1975

The world's population reaches 4 billion.

1986

The grain harvest for the world has grown to 1650 million tonnes, outstripping population growth.

1990s

Discovery that countries with high female literacy rates have low birth rates.

Racism & Genocide

AD 1933

OVERVIEW ❖ OVERVIEW ❖ OVERVIEW ❖ OVERVIEW ❖ OVERVIEW

The best known genocide is the killing of 6 million Jews by Nazi Germany, but many countries have given way to racial hatred and mass killings of this kind at various times in history. The Khmer Rouge regime in Cambodia was responsible for the deaths of 1.7 million Cambodians in the 1970s. Stalin's regime was guilty of the worst genocides known, the killing of 62 million people of various ethnic and national groups in the Soviet Union.

Poster for *The Eternal Jew*, a propaganda documentary produced by Goebbels which stirred up anti-Semitic violence.

Genocide is the systematic mass killing of a national or ethnic group. It has emerged as the greatest crime of the twentieth century, though it has gone on throughout human history, rooted as it is in racial hatred. The most highly publicized example is the persecution of the Jews by Nazi Germany, which began in the 1930s and escalated in the Second World War. The final phase of the Holocaust, as the mass killing of the Jews is known, began in December 1941, with the bureaucratically organized killing of Jews in death camps. The intention of the 'final solution' was the complete extermination of European Jewry. By 1945, the Germans had killed 6 million Jews.

1.7 million lost their lives in Cambodia in the 1970s, 21 percent of the country's population. As in Nazi Germany, East Timor, Guatemala, Yugoslavia and Rwanda, the Khmer Rouge regime led by Pol Pot combined extreme ideology with racial hatred. This led to cruelty and murder on a massive scale.

Over a million Armenians were killed by the Turks between 1880 and 1915. As Christians in a largely Muslim region, the Armenians were conspicuous, and attracted persecution for that reason. The Ottoman Empire planned their mass evacuation and extermination.

The largest democide, or mass killing of people in general, was by the Soviet Union under Stalin, who was responsible for the deaths of 62 million people. Some belonged to the wrong class, some to the wrong political faction, some to the wrong nation or ethnic group. Stalin was responsible for the deliberate starving to death of 5 million Ukrainian peasants in 1932-3. Stalin's crime was altogether greater in scale than Hitler's – 62 million compared with 21 million deaths. He was responsible for almost as many deaths as all the wars of the twentieth century put together.

An earlier genocide, of a different type, was the killing of Native Africans in the slave trade. An estimated 37 million black people died in slavery in the sixteenth to nineteenth centuries.

CHRONOLOGY OF EVENTS
AD 1500 – 1975

1500–1850

37 million Africans die in slavery.

1880–1915

Over a million Armenians are killed by the Turks.

1920s–50

62 million people are killed in the Soviet Union under Stalin.

1930s–45

Genocide of 6 million Jews across Europe under Hitler's regime.

1932–3

Stalin is responsible for the deliberate starving to death of 5 million Ukrainians.

1970s

1.7 million Cambodians are killed by Pol Pot 's regime in Cambodia.

Dec 1975

Indonesian troops begin genocide in East Timor.

Josef Stalin, 1879–1953, responsible for the deaths of over 62 million people.

Music: Experiments in Style

AD 1900

OVERVIEW ❖ OVERVIEW ❖ OVERVIEW ❖ OVERVIEW ❖ OVERVIEW

The twentieth century began with bold experiments, with composers inventing new musical scales, exploring new possibilities in harmony and orchestral colour. A great deal of music still looked back to the nationalism of the nineteenth century, feeding on folk songs and dances. The symphony too was made to do new things. An astonishing range of new music was written by great composers such as Debussy, Mahler, Stravinsky, Bartok, Puccini, Rachmaninov, Britten, Messiaen, Henze and Tippett.

Gustav Mahler 1860–1911.

At the start of the twentieth century, composers were looking for new modes of expression. Arnold Schoenberg (1874–1951) explored unusual harmonies, even throwing aside keys in favour of atonal music, which used all 12 notes of the scale to create melodies. Claude Debussy (1862–1918), who wrote *La Mer*, explored the possibilities of eastern music and created a style of music that was named after the movement in French painting that it resembled, Impressionism. Bela Bartok (1881–1945) and Ralph Vaughan Williams (1872–1958) continued the strong nationalist tendency of nineteenth century, using the folk music of their respective countries. Igor Stravinsky (1882) too drew on folk music, his *Rite of Spring* transforming Russian folk melody out of recognition with kaleidoscopic rhythms and vivid orchestral colours. Edgar Varese (1885–1965) explored the possibilities of rhythms rather than melodic or harmonic schemes. Jazz brought black American traditions into the mainstream; many classical composers have subsequently drawn on jazz idioms.

Somehow, the symphony survived this experimental period, though often transformed. Gustav Mahler (1860–1911) tried

Sergei Rachmaninov 1873–1943.

TIME LINE	40,000BC	10,000	5000	4000	500	AD1	200	4(

turning the traditional four movements into five, not just adding a choir for the final movement, like Beethoven, but vocal solos in earlier movements.

Giacomo Puccini 1858–1924.

Many of the twentieth century's greatest composers remained true to the traditional forms, such as Giacomo Puccini (1858–1924) and Sergei Rachmaninov (1873–1943), who were both unrepentent Romantics. Benjamin Britten (1913–1976), who wrote *Peter Grimes*, and Hans Werner Henze (1926–), who wrote *The Bassarids*, looked back to the world of nineteenth century opera. Michael Tippett (1905–1998), composing most influentially in the middle of the century, perhaps did most to liberate twentieth century composers from the often sterile experimentation of the early years of the century; he found clever new ways of developing melody by shifting keys so often that all sense of a home key vanished. Tippett also found ways of extending melody by a technique called 'additive rhythm', which sounds as free as jazz improvisation. His masterpiece is the opera *The Midsummer Marriage*.

Other composers, like Olivier Messiaen (1908–) and Toru Takemitsu (1930–1996), looked to the sounds of nature for their inspiration, or back to a simpler past where religion was at the centre of things, like John Tavener (1943–). In America, John Adams (1947–) has retreated to an age when public music was clear, strongly fashioned and immediately attractive. Philip Glass (1937–) has developed a minimalist style, which involves endless repetitions with only gradual variation.

CHRONOLOGY OF EVENTS
AD 1905 – 1993

1905	Claude Debussy: *La Mer*.
1905	Gustav Mahler: *Symphony No 6*.
1908	Sergei Rachmaninov: *Symphony No 2*.
1913	Igor Stravinsky: *Rite of Spring*.
1922	Ralph Vaughan Williams: *Pastoral Symphony*.
1926	Giacomo Puccini: *Turandot*.
1927	Edgar Varese: *Arcana*.
1932	Arnold Schoenberg: *Four Orchestral Songs*.
1933	Bela Bartok: *Piano Concerto No 2*.
1945	Benjamin Britten: *Peter Grimes*.
1955	Michael Tippett: *The Midsummer Marriage*.
1958	Olivier Messiaen: *Catalogue of Birds*.
1966	John Tavener: *The Whale*.
1978	John Adams: *Shaker Loops*.
1982	Toru Takemitsu: *Rain Coming*.
1992	Philip Glass: *The Voyage*.
1993	Hans Werner Henze: *Requiem*.

THE
TWENTY-FIRST
CENTURY

Doomsday Scenarios

AD 2000

OVERVIEW ❖ OVERVIEW ❖ OVERVIEW ❖ OVERVIEW ❖ OVERVIEW

As the Millennium approached, many people were gripped by an irrational fear that the world would end. Favourite doomsday scenarios were global warming and destruction by asteroids.

Global Warming

2002 was warmer than any other year in 120 years and, according to climate historians, probably the hottest for over 1200 years. World temperatures have risen one degree, from 14°C to 15°C, in the twentieth century. Some climatologists predict that they will rise another two degrees in the twenty-first century.

It is assumed that people are responsible for this global warming. A popular explanation is the release of ever-larger amounts of carbon dioxide by industries and vehicles. Carbon dioxide is a 'greenhouse gas', trapping the sun's heat.

But, if industrial growth really has been the cause, why was there cooling in the 1880s and 1970s, when industrialization continued? Other factors must be involved, such as variations in volcanic activity and solar radiation, and we have no control over these.

Global Ice Age

The present warm stage has lasted 10,000 years, and is probably nearly

Fears are that there will come a time when the sun will become too hot for life to continue on earth.

TIME LINE	40,000BC	10,000	5000	4000	500	AD1	200	40(

An asteroid collision would cause catastrophic damage to the earth. Astronomers are aware of a very low risk of such an event occurring in February 2019.

over. We may be about to plunge into another cold stage, bringing ice cover to North America, Northern Europe and Siberia. Studies of climate change in the past show that these changes can happen very fast.

Global warming could produce cooling on a continental scale. If the Arctic pack ice melts, the cold water released into the North Atlantic could block the Gulf Stream. Northern Europe would no longer be bathed in tropical water. Air temperatures in Britain would plunge 8°C, and the mountains would be covered in ice.

Asteroid Collisions

Astronomers tell us there are up to 1,000 large near-Earth objects at least 1km across. These pieces of debris are too small to see yet large enough to cause catastrophic damage if they collide with the Earth. The public perception is that the Earth could be hit by an asteroid at any moment.

Object NT7 is 2km across, big enough to cause continent-wide devastation. Its path brings it closest to the Earth on 1 February, 2019. Astronomers say that, although there is a risk of collision, it is a very low risk.

September 11: Global Terrorism

AD 2001

OVERVIEW ❖ OVERVIEW ❖ OVERVIEW ❖ OVERVIEW ❖ OVERVIEW

The Al Qaeda attack on Washington and New York on September 11, 2001, in which over 6,000 people died, represented an expression of frustration by Muslim extremists with the globalization originating in the West. Globalization replaces old ways of life with consumerism and the pursuit of wealth, which many traditional Muslims resist. The West wants to deal with the situation as a 'war against terrorism', but the underlying problem is a clash of civilizations.

September 11 and its consequences

On 11 September, 2001, a small group of Muslim extremists belonging to the Al Qaeda organization launched the world's worst terrorist attack on America. Three planes were hi-jacked and deliberately crashed into the Pentagon in Washington and the twin towers of the World Trade Centre in New York. Over 6,000 people were killed. The attack was organized by Osama bin Laden, then based in Afghanistan. Other equally unpredictable terrorist attacks have followed. On 12 October, 2001, Al Qaeda attacked a US warship: 17 American servicemen were killed.

Over 6,000 people, of many different nationalities, died in the terrorist attacks on September 11, 2001.

TIME LINE	40,000BC	10,000	5000	4000	500	AD1	200	40

On 12 October, 2002, a car bomb in Bali killed nearly 200 tourists, mainly young Australians.

The US government's response to the attacks was to declare war on terrorism. An attempt to capture Osama bin Laden by invading Afghanistan failed.

A clash of civilizations

The Cold War has been succeeded by a more dangerous clash of civilizations. Islam embraces a vision of a religion-based society. The West has in the main left behind its religious belief in favour of individual freedom and democracy. 70 percent of the world's refugees are Muslims fleeing from repression in Muslim countries, and ironically many of them hate the freedom and consumerism of the western societies they now find themselves living in.

Many Muslims feel that their culture is threatened by the invasiveness of globalization.

The policies of the West in the Middle East over several decades have increasingly frustrated Muslims. The way the international community has allowed the Israelis to go on taking land from Palestinians has been a provocation, but Palestinian leader Yasser Arafat rejects Osama bin Laden's claim that the Palestinian cause is Al Qaeda's cause. He accuses bin Laden of opportunism.

The war against terrorism continued in March 2003 with a coalition invasion, led by America and the United Kingdom, of Iraq. The declared aim of this invasion was to uncover the weapons of mass destruction believed to be held by Saddam Hussein. This invasion resulted in the overthrow of Saddam's brutal regime and has therefore precipitated change in the political map of the Middle East. Terrorist attacks however, continue to threaten the world.

CHRONOLOGY OF EVENTS
AD 1990 – 2003

2 Aug 1990

Iraqi troops invade Kuwait.

19 Aug 1990

Iraq deports foreign nationals in Kuwait to use as 'human shields' at military installations in Iraq, anticipating attack.

16 Jan 1991

Operation Desert Storm, the Gulf War, begins. The declared US aim is to liberate Kuwait.

28 Feb 1991

President Bush (Senior) announces suspension of hostilities in Kuwait and Iraq.

11 Sep 2001

Al Qaeda attack the Pentagon in Washington and the World Trade Centre in New York, killing over 6000 people.

12 Oct 2001

Al Qaeda attack a US warship: 17 American servicemen killed.

12 Oct 2002

A car bomb in Bali kills nearly 200 tourists.

2002

Palestinian leader Yasser Arafat rejects Osama bin Laden's claim that the Palestinian cause is Al Qaeda's cause. He accuses bin Laden of opportunism.

Feb 2003

President Bush (Junior) orders an invasion on Iraq, prompting fears of new terrorist attacks on the West.

INDEX

PICTURE ACKNOWLEDGEMENTS

Bridgeman Art Library: 12, 23, 27, 35, 59, 73, 85, 109, 146, 154, 176, 178, 231

Freefoto.Com: 14, 67, 83, 84, 97, 99, 103, 111, 119, 124, 129, 132, 141, 141, 143, 145, 153, 158, 171, 191, 202, 203, 210, 219

Getty Images: 48, 49, 52, 103, 152, 158, 172, 180, 190, 209, 215, 228, 248, 250

Courtesy of the artist, Graham Turner (www.studio88.co.uk): 86

Mary Evans Picture Library: 13, 17, 18, 19, 20, 21, 22, 24, 28, 30, 34, 36, 38, 39, 42, 46, 50, 57, 58, 60, 64, 68, 69, 75, 76, 79, 81, 81, 83, 91, 92, 93, 94, 98, 105 106, 107, 108, 111, 114, 117, 118, 120, 121, 122, 123, 126, 129, 131, 134, 136, 137, 140, 144, 147, 151, 153, 155, 157, 159, 160, 161, 163, 168, 169, 178, 179, 181, 182, 183, 184, 185, 185, 186, 188, 189, 198 199, 200, 204, 205, 207, 208, 212, 213, 216, 217, 217, 218, 222, 229, 232, 233, 239, 242, 243, 244, 244, 244

Mirrorpix: 238